The U.S. in Prophecy

All Scripture quotations are from the King James Version of the Holy Bible.

Parts of this book were originally written by S. Franklin Logsdon and published by Zondervan Publishing House.

Printed in the United States of America

ISBN 1-57558-060-8

The U.S.
in
Prophecy

Dr. Noah Hutchings
S. Franklin Logsdon

America! America!
God mend thy every flaw;
Confirm thy soul in self-control,
Thy liberty in law.

Table of Contents

Introduction

In 1968 Zondervan Publishing Company published a book by Dr. S. Franklin Logsdon titled *The U.S.A. in Prophecy*. This was indeed a bold venture by Zondervan, even though the author was well known and respected. Dr. Logsdon served as pastor of the church named for its founder, Dwight L. Moody, a church known at that time for its fundamental and evangelical foundations. Dr. Logsdon had also worked for the Lockman Foundation in bringing forth the NASB, one of the more contemporary versions of the Bible at the time. However, it is fair to note that Dr. Logsdon later expressed regrets for having a part in this scriptural translation project and returned to using the King James Version.

Nevertheless, Dr. Logsdon risked his reputation by daring to declare that the Babylon of Revelation 18, a great nation represented by a principal city, was none other than our beloved United States — America upon which God has shed His grace, even from sea to shining sea. How dare this ecclesiastical Benedict Arnold prophesy that this God-blessed land would be destroyed as Sodom and Gomorrah in one day? Especially was this theory untenable since the United States was trying to survive a nuclear threat and future national uncertainty in the midst of the Cold War with Russia, as well as suffering the throes of a humiliating war in Vietnam.

However, *The U.S.A. in Prophecy* by Logsdon was published, and Zondervan over the next several years reprinted the book nine times. Although we do not have the exact number of copies published, we must assume it ran into the hundreds of thousands. At some point in the late seventies Zondervan ceased publication of the book. It is not known to me why publication ceased, as it evidently was continuing to be sold in Christian bookstores. After the departure of Pat Zondervan from the company and the entrance of other interests (including Rupert Murdoch), the publishing policy of Zondervan Publishing changed. Zondervan also came out with the New International Version of the Bible and may have wanted to phase out books that used KJV references.

I came into possession of a copy of *The U.S.A. in Prophecy* by Logsdon in the early seventies. While I did not accept with great zeal the premise that our country was the Babylon of Revelation 18, I did think that it was a good study and worthy of consideration. In the late seventies, in attempting to find an extra copy for a friend, Edward Tracy, I discovered that it was out of stock and no reprinting was being considered. Therefore, I made a copy and sent the one I had to Brother Tracy. Edward Tracy had revived my interest in the U.S.-Babylon theory, and he even wrote a sequel to Dr. Logsdon's book. Brother Tracy in 1990 was slowly dying of Lou Gehrig's disease, so I visited him at his home located in the mountains of California between Sutter's Mill and Lake Tahoe. This was a few weeks before Brother Tracy was called home to be with the Lord.

In March 2000, Hearthstone Publishing confronted me with a proposition regarding writing a new book on the subject of the United States in prophecy. After much searching, we located the mimeographed copy of Dr. Logsdon's book. We contacted Zondervan and were told that the copyright had run out and the company had no further interest in the book, and we could have it.

In 1990, I had written a book titled *The Persian Gulf Crisis* about ancient Babylon and the modern role of Saddam Hussein in invading Kuwait, threatening the peace of the region and the security of sixty percent of the world's oil. Twenty thousand copies of my book came off the press in November 1990 and ten thousand copies were sold in December. But then in January, there was a seventy-two–hour war. Interest in the book immediately dissolved. After all, no one wanted a book about a war that never actually happened. Nevertheless, in my book was much valuable history and contemporary research about Babylon. So Hearthstone staff lifted information from my book that applied to Babylon, butted it up against Dr. Logsdon's book, and asked me work on it.

Going back to 1968, we might wonder why a scholar like Dr. Logsdon would go off on a tangent and present the unpopular opinion that the U.S. was Babylon. But the 1960s were the decade of the "flower children"—the hippies; the dropout generation; free love; if it feels good, do it; flag burners; Jane Fonda in Hanoi and Bill Clinton in Moscow; and hundreds like them trying to bring down our government while aiding and abetting our enemies. Theologians were preaching that God is dead, and so-called Christian leaders like James Pike were searching for the bones of Jesus in the Judean desert. In the meantime there was the U.S. military war in Vietnam, and the Russians threatening to nuke the U.S. into oblivion. All this was happening while our courts were pushing God out of education and our music and art both looked and sounded like a thousand cats fighting, or worse. It is small wonder that a man of God after the heart of Jeremiah would conclude that this must be the Babylon of Revelation.

In 1972, four years after Dr. Logsdon wrote *The U.S.A. in Prophecy,* an announcement appeared in the media — Babylon in Iraq was going to be restored to its former estate. WOW! What a prophetic bombshell!

In 1978, I led a tour of one hundred three members to several countries in the Middle East, which included Iraq, and a visit to personally witness the rebuilding of Babylon. This experience I discuss in full detail in the last half of this book. The opinion that the United States was Babylon faded away, at least for a time. Of course, there were some difficulties in that Iraq was a small country and the Euphrates was a rather shallow winding stream and could in no way fulfill the description of the Babylon in Revelation 18. But what if Iraq did conquer all the Middle East oil fields? Considering the Panama Canal and the Volga Waterway, making Babylon a major seaport would be a piece of cake. But with the war with Iran and the Desert Storm military operation, and continuing U.S.– U.N. military and economic restrictions, the idea of Babylon's restoration to its former glory began to fade also.

Babylon, the city, is no mystery, either historically or in a contemporary setting. The Babylon of Revelation 17 and 18 is a mystery. Perhaps no one, including Dr. Logsdon and myself, has completely uncovered this mystery. But this is what makes a mystery fascinating and intriguing.

Dr. Logsdon with great intensity, aggressively and without compromise, presents the United States as the Babylon of Revelation 18. In my half of the book, I take a calmer and more analytic approach to the subject. But who knows? Before I write the concluding chapter, perhaps I too will agree with Dr. Logsdon on the identity of the scripturally unrevealed country.

Part One presents the dissertation of Dr. Logsdon written in 1968. We may wonder if Dr. Logsdon would have changed or modified any opinions had he waited until 1973 to write his book. We will not make changes in the author's copy. Just keep in mind that the first half of this book was written in 1968.

Part Two presents parts from the book I wrote in 1990,

just six weeks before the Desert Storm War. Updates and new chapters constitute an appraisal and hopefully an objective conclusion, that considers all the facts and evidence relating to the United States as the Babylon of Revelation 18. Whether these conclusions are accepted or rejected by the reader, I believe this book does contain the most pervasive study on this subject in print.

Part One
Is the U.S.A. in Prophecy?

by S. Franklin Logsdon

Chapter 1

Looking Ahead

"We will bury you!"

Thus roared Nikita Khrushchev in the epithet of the ages, as he poured forth one of his innumerable invectives against the U.S.A. To most Americans it was but the outburst of an irresponsible individual, scarcely worthy of notice, and was met with lightness and even laughter.

But let us not forget that Mr. Khrushchev was speaking as the leader of the increasingly powerful Soviet Union. Representing as he was the avowed enemy of the United States, there is no doubt he was reflecting the feeling, if not the united intent, of his compatriots. Nor is there any reason to believe, with the passing of Khrushchev from the scene, that the Soviets have abandoned, or even lessened, their insidious animosity and hostility against our country. The subsiding of the Cold War is definitely a matter of expediency.* It is in the best interests for the Russian bear to let up on his growling in order to gain grain. It is only a change of stance, not a change of philosophy or design.

The threatening sentence by Mr. Khrushchev has all but

---

*Keep in mind this was written in 1968.

faded from the minds of our citizenry — dismissed as exorbitant language or even as a tyranny of words. Our only point in calling the reader's attention to it is that it possibly may prove, when the facts are assembled, to coincide with the authoritative prophecy of the infinite God Himself. And this is the burden of this treatise.

This presentation, however, is no attempt to be spectacular, no giddy excursion into sheer fantasy. It is simply a bold endeavor to face up to some staggering and alarming suggestions, an exploration of solemn and serious portents. Just what does the future hold for this great nation which, in less than two hundred years, grew from a handful of immigrants into the wealthiest, most powerful nation of all time? But our ship of state is in turbulent waters. Is it headed for some disastrous shoals? The precipitant end of an errant course? Can someone tell us?

The prognosticator has been around a long while, even from time immemorial. His voice is heard in every area of human concern. Those with recognized expertise in discerning developments are in demand by all branches of the news media. They are heard on panel discussions, listened to in public lectures, and read in periodicals. They are asked for information pertaining to industrial production, the financial outlook, and business possibilities. Cataclysmic changes in this fast-moving world can disappoint the most popular forecaster or diviner, but the Bible, on the other hand, is immutable, inexorable. It never changes. When we rest upon it, we can be certain of stability and permanence.

But we must be reminded that prophecy is both perceptive and predictive — predictive when the conclusions are obscured; perceptive when the conclusions are obvious. That is to say, man can predicate certain forecasts on the basis of conditions or signs. Jesus said to the Pharisees, "When it is evening, ye say, It will be fair weather, for the sky is red." Weather conditions, economic tendencies, business trends, even epidemics can be foretold with some accuracy on the strength of certain portending signs.

The predictive realm is a different picture entirely. The future is locked away in the omniscience of Deity. It is hidden completely from the eyes of man. What it holds, what it will bring forth, must await the gradual unfolding of time. That is, unless the One who is omniscient chooses to reveal it through His biblical record. This, of course, He has done in a great many instances, and concerning a great number of matters. But has He said anything specific about the United States?

There is, understandably, mounting concern over prevailing conditions, such as the Watergate scandal, the energy crisis, unemployment, inflation, pollution, increasing crime, the explosive situation in the Middle East, and international problems as they relate directly or indirectly to us. This leads people to inquire about the future. With greater frequency than ever before, the question is being posed, What does Bible prophecy say about our God-honored and greatly blessed nation?

The prevailing attitude in this connection seems to be, not that God has not spoken, but where and how has He spoken? How may one know?

Credibility in the Bible may be strengthened in the minds of those not too conversant with it if we cite a few convincing facts. The Bible was miraculously inspired through some forty men who, for the most part, never met one another, who lived in different places in different eras, yet it possesses an unimpeachable unity throughout. Its circulation has dwarfed all other publications. Its appeal continues. Our system of jurisprudence is firmly founded upon it, and all our finer ethical and moral principles have been derived from the days of yore, that even in these times of declining religious professions, differing philosophies, and opposing forces, leaders being inducted into high offices in our land are still required to place their hand on the Bible in order to be sworn in.

But more pertinent to the subject before us, it is interesting to know that biblical predictions are fulfilled with letter-perfect exactitude and with never a failure. This cannot be said about human forecasts. For an example, in point, there were forty specific predictions made in the Old Testament about the crucifixion of Christ, some as far back as fifteen hundred years beforehand. All forty were minutely fulfilled within one day. According to the law of compound probabilities, the chance that they "happened" together by "accident" is too remote for any intelligent person to believe. By human prognostication, these forty prophecies would have rated only one in two trillion chances of fulfillment. Thus, if it can be established that the Bible has something to say specifically about our country, we may with confidence bank upon the veracity of the information.

If God has spoken on any matter in the Bible, it is because He wants humankind to know about it. It is not an enigma. Revelation is for information, but the whole revelation on a given matter may not necessarily be found in one context. One of the basic laws of hermeneutics is that Scripture must be compared with Scripture. In this manner of collecting and collating, the pieces can be put in their proper places, causing the picture to emerge clearly and convincingly.

We launch into the subject at hand with the comfortable assumption that the omniscient God, looking down the corridors of time, and concerning Himself so prominently with the Gentile nations, did not overlook the one nation He blessed above all others. We proceed logically and reasonably to extract from the biblical account the description of an unnamed nation. Then, deductively, giving careful attention to relationships, endeavors, accomplishments, and character, we shall press toward a crystallization for identification.

We will observe the tendencies and trends of national behavior on the part of a particular nation, one singularly blessed, which incurs the displeasure and eventual indignation of the Most High God, and how she places herself in line for His severe judgment. She diminishes in world influence and deteriorates internally. Boasting of superb power and mighty defenses and fantastic scientific development, but living lustfully and godlessly, she finally plunges into desolation.

Even perceptive prediction finds much current encouragement toward a rather bleak forecast, with so many alarming portents on the horizon and perturbing omens multiplying constantly. Frank Goble of the Thomas Jefferson Research Center has stated: "Unless our schools and society are able to find far better and more economical solutions to exploding human crises, we face social and economic chaos. The situation is worse than most Americans realize. Virtually every crisis is out of control." Mr. Goble particularly referred to the "crisis of confidence" in our educational system, in our political process, in our monetary system, etc.

Peaceful coexistence has become a colloquialism. It has become an unpardonable excuse for toleration in those areas where subversives threaten the peace and good fortune of our whole society. The church is not excepted. Too long have we figured we could contain the enemy by a detente, by professing but not practicing godliness. Out of the "goodness" of our hearts we have encouraged peaceful coexistence by welcoming into our church life and program symbols of enemy dress, sounds of his distracting music, and sentiments of his undignified terminology until confusion is as thick as the morning fog on the Gulf of Mexico.

The proverbial camel has intruded more than his ominous head into our sacred precincts. Now, we are confronted with the fact that the unwholesome intruder cannot be expelled, because the weaklings in the flock have learned to love the wolf in sheep's clothing, and the shepherds are not sufficiently disposed to cast him out. And the nation's problems are similar in nature. Watergate, the energy crisis, the stock market decline, unemployment, inflation, with suspense and fear, are casting a pall over our country which has been dashing inordinately toward some kind of precipice.

Lenin, in pleading for loyalty to the communist cause, said, "A successful revolution cannot be had through a part-time endeavor."

America, take note! If all our resources, unexcelled privileges, and the blessings of freedom are to be enjoyed, if our children, even those yet unborn, are to have this great heritage, spiritual decadence, and patriotic deterioration must be stemmed and reversed. There must be a renaissance of devotion to that which is worthwhile and promising, but such revivals are not readily produced. Some would rather drift than strive. Said Dr. Paul Rees, "America must be stabbed awake. The blackness of the blackest night is settling about us. The blackest part of the picture is the inaction and lack of conviction on the part of those who should have the proper vision."

Israel in the long ago sowed to the wind and reaped the whirlwind (Hos. 8:7). And the winds of adversity still pack a powerful punch for present-day Israel. How awesome and terrifying may be the final result of America's careless course. This should become apparent in the following pages.

Chapter 2

Is the U.S.A. in Prophecy?

Now to the point. If you ask, Is the U.S.A. mentioned by name in prophecy? the answer, of course, is "no." But, if you ask, Is the U.S.A. in the framework of prophecy? the answer is an unqualified "yes," as the following Bible references will reveal. These references are clearly and distinctly universal in scope, and therefore embrace the U.S.A. This fact established, in due course, we may move from the general to the specific in an attempt to focus the spotlight of prophecy upon a single nation which may prove to be the United States of America.

1. In a panoramic declaration of prophetic intention, God says, "This is the purpose that is purposed upon the whole earth" (Isa. 14:26). The U.S.A. obviously is part of the "whole earth" and would have to be in the framework of prophecy.

2. The above reference continues, "and this is the hand that is stretched out upon all the nations." Of course, the U.S.A. is one of the "all nations."

3. "Though I make a full end of all nations whither I have scattered thee, yet will I not make a full end of thee [Israel]" (Jer. 30:11).

   Israel is the only nation with which the infinite God

has had a vital relationship (Amos 3:2), and it will be restored to divine blessing and usefulness. All other nations
will lose their sovereign identity. Meanwhile, the Jews are
scattered among many nations. These nations, the text
states, will come to a "full end."

The U.S.A. has a great number of these dispersed Jews.
Since it is declared that all such nations will come to an
end, therefore, the U.S.A. will have her national existence
terminated by the hand of God — sometime.

4. "I will execute vengeance in anger and fury upon the heathen [none excepted], such as they have not heard" (Mic.
5:15). This is a prophesied judgment which will strike when
rebellion against divine authority becomes prevalent. Fast
becoming spiritually decadent, the U.S.A. is apparently included in the above prophecy.

5. "And all the heathen shall see my judgment . . ." (Ezek.
39:21). Here again, we note the all-inclusive adjective.
Where is there the slightest glimmer of assurance that our
country can possibly escape the fearful consequences of
forgetting and forsaking God who has lavished upon us
His abounding goodness and lovingkindness?

6. "For the day of the LORD is near upon all the heathen . . .
and they shall be as though they had not been" (Obad. 15–
16). This is a declarative statement, authentic, authoritative, and prophetic. There is no indication of an exception.

7. "And I will overthrow the throne of kingdoms, and I will
destroy the strength of the kingdoms of the heathen . . ."
(Hag. 2:22). The context clearly states that this prophecy
is yet future — how far beyond contemporary times is not
known. There seems to be no comfortable reason to think
that it cannot be comparatively soon.

8. ". . . I have put my spirit upon him [Christ]: he shall bring
forth judgment to the Gentiles" (Isa. 42:1). God does not
say that a single nation shall be exempt, so this prophecy

must include the U.S.A.

9. "The lion is come up from his thicket, and the destroyer of the Gentiles is on his way . . ." (Jer. 4:7). The lion coming up from his thicket, and the "adversary the devil, as a roaring lion" (1 Pet. 5:8) are expressions of prevailing lawlessness and rampant godlessness. This, according to the prophecy, signals the soon coming of the Lord to put down all rebellion. He will then "destroy" the nations. Once again, there is no exception. Thus, the U.S.A. would have to be included.

10. "Why do the heathen rage, and the people imagine a vain thing? . . . He that sitteth in the heavens shall laugh: the Lord shall have them in derision" (Ps. 2:1, 4). The word "rage" means "to be tumultuous," and springs from a root suggesting commotion, restlessness, disquietude, noise, and trouble. The thought is, What do the nations expect to gain through tumultuous demonstrations and widespread commotion, through rioting and noise? These conditions are commonplace in America.

Actually, it is unthinkable that the God who knows the end from the beginning would pinpoint such small nations as Libya, Egypt, Ethiopia, and Syria in the prophetic declaration and completely overlook the wealthiest and most powerful nation on the earth. Too long have we evaded the question. Too long have we summarily grouped our country with the so-called revived Roman Empire. Too long have we persisted in terming the U.S.A. in prophecy as one of the "lion's cubs," thus giving her but an inferential mention in the shadow of a diminishing Britain.

Chapter 3

Identifying Unspecified Entities

Man seems to have a special delight and a strong aptitude for the use of nicknames and symbolical terms. A glossary of such terms would make a voluminous volume indeed, and would be interesting as well. Of course, they would have to be grouped in their related categories. Perhaps the sportscasters and sportswriters are the most gifted in this art.

The Bambino would of course be the homerun-swatting Babe Ruth of some years back, with *The Hammer,* Henry Aaron, the current champion in that category. Everyone conversant with boxing would recognize the *Brown Bomber* as Joe Louis. The *gridiron* is the football field, the *diamond* the baseball field, and the *ring* (though it is square) the place of contest for the pugilists. But nowhere do figurative appellations abound as in the Scriptures. And the difficulty is that people, conversant in many other areas, have failed to acquaint themselves with the language of the Bible.

Prophetic entities, not specifically named in the Bible, may be identified by representations or by descriptions. Christ as the King of righteousness is represented by Melchisedec, to whom Abraham of old paid tithes in the way. The northern kingdom of Israel (ten tribes) is represented by Ephraim. Dispersed Israel is represented by Loammi, the son of the prophet Hosea. Elijah is represented by John the Baptist as the forerunner of Christ. The devil is represented by the term *old dragon*. These are but a few illustrations, but sufficient to establish our point.

Descriptions in the Bible are even more numerous than representations. Metaphors and similes abound. They sparkle with appropriate grandeur when setting forth the Son of God who came in human flesh to be the Savior of the world. He is described as the seed of the woman, the virgin-born, the ancient of days, the Lamb of God, the door, the bread of life, the light of the world, the righteous servant, the branch, the bright and morning star, the water of life, the second man, the last Adam, to mention a few.

The devil, too, is set forth in the Scriptures by myriads of descriptions. He is referred to as the serpent, the lying spirit, the son of the morning, the deceiver, the tempter, the enemy, the unclean spirit, the foul spirit, the angel of light, the angel of the bottomless pit, the great dragon, the old serpent, the accuser, the murderer, the liar, and the father of lies.

The church, composed of all true believers in Christ wherever they may be found, is spoken of as a building, a bride, and a body, suggesting in a broad sense the matter of communion, the fact of companionship, and the thought of commission. The great doctrines of the New Testament are built around these aspects of Christian profession.

The coming world dictator, so irrefutably established in biblical revelation, is set forth as the little horn, the king, the man of sin, the son of perdition, the wicked one, the Antichrist, and the beast. And in no other area of holy writ has there been more speculation. His exact identity, in terms of contemporary individuals, has often been attempted with embarrassing futility. He is to have a name with the numerical value of its letters amounting to 666.

Then, it is interesting also to note how proper names are used as descriptive designations or as marks of identification. The word "Baalim" is employed for idolatry, "David" for the Lord Jesus Christ, the "swelling of the Jordan" for emergencies, even for death itself, and "Jerusalem that is above" meaning heaven.

If you were to ask the simple question, Where was Jesus crucified? would you be surprised if the apostle John were to tell you it was in Sodom and Egypt? Would you charge him with ambiguity? Or would you accuse him of a lapse of memory? Perhaps you would declare him somewhat senile. Well, in the Revelation, the last book in the Bible, in chapter eleven, verse eight, this is what he wrote: "The great city, which spiritually is called Sodom and Egypt, where also our Lord was crucified." The proper nouns are used descriptively and not designatively, Sodom being a symbol of wickedness, and Egypt meaning unspiritual in character.

Thus, if Jerusalem, the city of peace, is given such unbelievable descriptive appellations in the Bible, it should not surprise us to discover a strange noun to describe the U.S.A. in prophecy. And let us here point out that the chief reason the United States is not listed by name in the Scriptures is simply and obviously because it was not in existence in Bible days. The writers did not know the ethnic name. The same is true of the prophesied world dictator. He was not in existence when the predictions were given, so he is only described until he takes his place in the developing order of things. When he comes, all the descriptions will fit him. And since the U.S.A. is now in existence, there must be descriptions to fit her if she is discoverable in the framework of prophecy.

We must, therefore, search for designations or descriptions or both, which in a convincing manner are applicable. By description, we can identify people, places, and things. Thus, it should not be impossible, or even difficult to identify a nation in this manner.

As a lecturer, traveling far and wide for many years, I have been met on many occasions at the airport. Writing ahead to the one in charge of plans, I have invariably stated, "If I am unknown to the one designated to meet me at the plane, I can be identified as a man without a hat and carrying a gold-colored suitbag." The individual, of course, as the passengers deplane one by one, would be looking for the given description. When one emerges without a hat and carrying a gold-colored suitbag, he would naturally conclude, "There he is," and would make his approach and introduction.

Our task now, and it is a most interesting one, is to search for the descriptions of a nation. It has to be a modern nation, one that was utterly unknown in ancient times. The search will not be in vain.

A Probable Lead

We need to have etched upon our minds a very prominent teaching in the Bible which may lend assistance in the pursuance of our subject. It is the *Babylon doctrine.* It involves infinitely more than the casual Bible reader would imagine. Emerging in the tenth chapter of Genesis, it extends to the nineteenth chapter of Revelation and that takes us through almost the entire Bible. It actually commences with a man by the name of Nimrod, about whom it is said, "He began to be a mighty one in the earth" (Gen. 10:8).

Thus, beginning in the days of Nimrod in the early chapters of the Bible and continuing through the Scriptures to the heavenly "hallelujahs" of final defeat in Revelation 19, the Babylon doctrine has an impressive place. The word "Babylon" is synonymous with confusion, and Satan is its author (1 Cor. 14:33). It is, in one form or another, a diabolical attempt to contradict all that God says and to counteract all that He does.

This Babylonian matter is comprehended within three designations: (1) *Historical Babylon* in Genesis 11; (2) *Ecclesiastical Babylon* in Revelation 17; and (3) *Political Babylon* in Revelation 18. Historical Babylon will ultimately manifest itself in two imposing branches, viz., the false church and a powerful God-forsaking nation. These will suffer defeat at the hands of Him who will not tolerate ungodly usurpation of His royal rights and divine prerogatives.

Historical Babylon is symbolized by a monumental tower, *ecclesiastical Babylon* by a mystical woman, and *political Babylon* by a mighty city. The aim is, respectively, to reach heaven, to rob heaven, and to reject heaven. The proposal of the first was a common language. The proposal of the second is a common worship. The proposal of the third is a common privilege — one speech, one church, one society. The Utopian dream, in each instance, may be expressed as (1) a cohesion of people, (2) a commingling of churches, and (3) a confluence of power — to stay together, to worship together, to excel all others.

In the case of historical Babylon, God felled the tower, confounded the tongues, and scattered the people.

In the case of ecclesiastical or religious Babylon, the beast (Antichrist) will hate the "harlot" (meaning the false church), outlaw religion, and finally kill the "woman"; that is, he will destroy the final development of organized religion.

In the case of prophesied political Babylon, trials will plague the earth, the economy will crash, the great city will be made desolate. See chart on following page.

The alert reader will have sensed the many suggested involvements in this highly condensed outline. Building a tower to reach heaven suggests the blatant doctrine of "salvation by works" — the age-long claim that, "If I do the best I can, or if I keep the Ten Commandments, or if I observe the golden rule,

THE CONFUSION AND CONFOUNDING OF BABYLON			
"Babylon the Great is fallen, is fallen" (Rev. 14:8).			
DESIGNATION	**SYMBOL**	**PROPOSAL**	**UTOPIAN DREAM**
Historical "B" (Gen. 11)	A Monumental Tower To Reach Heaven	A Common Language One Speech	Cohesion of People To Stay Together
Ecclesiastical "B" (Rev. 17)	A Mystical Woman To Rob Heaven	A Common Worship One Church	Commingling of Churches To Get Together
Political "B" (Rev. 18)	A Mighty City To Reject Heaven	A Common Privilege One Society	Confluence of Power To Excel All Others
Defeated "B" (1 Cor. 15:25)	God Fells the Tower Beast Hates Harlot Trials Plague Earth	Tongues Confounded Religion Outlawed Economy Crashes	People Are Scattered Woman Is Killed City Is Made Desolate
HISTORICAL BABYLON eventuates in	Religious Babylon — The False Church (Rev. 17) Political Babylon — The Great Nation (Rev. 18)		

I'm sure I'll reach heaven at last." This is a clear contradiction of the authoritative Word of God. "For by grace are ye saved through faith; and that not of yourselves: it is the gift of God: Not of works, lest any man should boast" (Eph. 2:8–9).

Babylonism is not only a system of contradictory works, but a scheme of unmitigated robbery, depriving the infinite God of the praise and glory due His holy name, denying His power and His operations. Babylonism is also a satanic willfulness which rejects divine intervention and seeks to solve its own problems and to build its own arrangement of things, giving no thought to God's will or way. This is termed "interpersonal theology." "The world *we* are building" is a current expression, illustrative of this present climate or attitude.

The proposal is that of a one-church, one-world development, which, through ecumenicity, unionization, common markets, and the U.N., is currently gaining rapid momentum. It will all culminate in the religionist's fondest dream and in the Devil's amazing success — the ultimate in monumental unbelief among men. But "he that sitteth in the heavens shall laugh: the Lord shall have them in derision" (Ps. 2:4).

God, who established His battalions in the skies, from before the foundation of the world, has set the exact time for each of His inevitable victories of these forces of unrighteousness. He will eliminate utterly the false church through the agency of Antichrist or the coming world dictator (Rev. 17:17). He will also completely destroy a powerful end-time nation which is spiritually called Babylon (Rev. 18:18). The word "end-time" connotes the closing days of the present order of things.

There will be an eternal memorial to Christ's complete triumph over Babylon's deception and tyranny, both in the religious and political realms. This will occasion the second greatest of all celebrations (the greatest being the exhibition of the redeemed church as recorded in Ephesians 2:7) as a thunderous chorus jubilantly cries, "Alleluia! for the Lord God omnipotent reigneth" (Rev. 19:6).

A Search for the Key

Now, we will explore the possibility of finding a key in this Babylon doctrine as we search for the answer to the question, Is the U.S.A. in prophecy? Admittedly, there are some problems to be encountered, but they are not too difficult to solve. The first one we meet is the plurality of applications for the word "Babylon." The following may offer some clarification:

Historical Babylon — a system
Political Babylon — an empire
Municipal Babylon — a city
Prophetical Babylon — a) the world church, and
b) an end-time nation

It would be even more difficult meeting these plural applications were it not for the fact that such situations are found in many other areas of scriptural consideration. As an illustration in point, the word "world" has various connotations in

Scripture. The context, however, always indicates whether the meaning is (1) the sphere on which we live, or (2) the human family which God so loved that He gave His only Son, that whosoever believeth in Him should never perish, or (3) the satanic system which is designed to keep people content without God, and which the believer is not to love (1 John 2:15).

The context should enable us to ascertain the proper application of the word "Babylon." We will know whether the Holy Spirit is referring to historical, political, municipal, or prophetical Babylon. If this were not true, we would face hopeless confusion in trying to discern prophetical declarations.

The second obstacle which presents itself is this: Is prophetical Babylon a nation or a city? In Jeremiah 50 and 51, it is presented as a nation; in Revelation 18, it is a city. But there is no contradiction, indeed cannot be! Nations are referred to by the chief or capital city. Thus, we speak of Washington for the U.S.A., Moscow for Russia, Paris for France, London for England, Saigon for South Vietnam, etc.

The *Journal Herald* of Toledo, Ohio, May 14, 1968, captioned its report of Vietnam peace talks in Paris in this manner: "WASHINGTON AND HANOI ARE SEATED AT THE TABLE." When Jesus cried out, "O Jerusalem, Jerusalem!" He clearly meant the nation. A few Bible quotations will suffice to prove that prophetical Babylon is a nation:

". . . How is Babylon become a desolation among the nations!" (Jer. 50:23).

". . . Shall empty her land . . ." (Jer. 51:2).

"Her cities are a desolation. . . " (Jer. 51:43).

". . . I will punish the king of Babylon and his land . . ." (Jer. 50:18).

The parent verse for the Revelation 18 references to Babylon as a city is found in Jeremiah 51:6, in which context it is irrefutably a nation. Thus, prophetical Babylon is a nation and not a city.

The third problem to be faced in attempting to find a key in the Babylon doctrine is that of determining whether or not the Babylon prophecies in Jeremiah 50 and 51 actually project into the remote future — to what is commonly called "the end-time."

Much prophecy has a near and a distant application. All must agree to this. But some claim that all references to Babylon in these Jeremiah chapters are historical in character; hence, already fulfilled. Others maintain that there is convincing, even irrefutable, evidence of remote prophecy in these Jeremiah chapters — much that to this date definitely has not been fulfilled. Proof of this latter claim is most relevant to our consideration. Ponder the following:

> In those days, and in that time, saith the LORD, the children of Israel shall come, they and the children of Judah together, going and weeping: they will go, and seek the LORD their God. . . . In those days, and in that time, saith the LORD, the iniquity [rebellion] of Israel shall be sought for, and there shall be none.
>
> — Jeremiah 50:4, 20

These prophecies, beyond any possibility of contradiction, are of future fulfillment when the promised regathering and restoration will find Israel and Judah (once and for so long a time divided) reunited and reconciled to Jehovah-God in the land which was promised them through Abraham. There is an impressive number of such evidences of remote prophecy in these Jeremiah chapters.

This fact of unfulfilled prophecies in Jeremiah 50 and 51 finds some strong support in the divinely-employed expression "daughter of Babylon" (Jer. 51:33). Daughter of which Babylon? The Babylonian Empire had no offspring as will the Roman Empire. The city had no prophesied successor. It is and must of necessity be understood to be the daughter or outgrowth of historical Babylon — that system of the ages with its God-rejecting tendencies and sacrilegious influences which, in the end-time, will eventuate in two imposing branches, namely, *religious* Babylon, the ultimate of organized religious systems, and *political* or *economic* Babylon, a nation of impressive and superior characteristics.

A corollary to bolster this "daughter" suggestion may be found in Jeremiah 4:31 where God speaks of the "daughter of Zion." Notice the similarity of expression. God was referring to the descendants of those whom He was then addressing. He was pointing out their sorrow and their woes, and the application carries through to contemporary times, and even to a time yet in the future. The quotation reads as follows:

> For I have heard a voice as of a woman in travail, and the anguish as of her that bringeth forth her first child, the voice of the daughter of Zion, that bewaileth herself, that spreadeth her hands, saying, Woe is me now! for my soul is wearied because of murderers.
>
> — Jeremiah 4:31

Because God knew the end from the beginning, and the people did not, He pointed out to them the painful consequences their rebellion against Him would visit upon their descendants. Way back there in antiquity, God dipped into the future and revealed that He heard their posterity moaning and groaning under anti-Semitic persecution. He heard every moan of the five hundred thousand who starved to death in Poland. He heard every pitiful cry of the six million who perished under the heel of Hitler.

When the facts of prophecy are properly and understandingly viewed in Jeremiah 50 and 51, what God says about the "daughter of Babylon" is just as clear as that which He reveals about the "daughter of Zion." And observe, the word "daughter" is in the singular. There are two extensions of Babylon — the religious and the political. The context makes it clear that the reference here to "daughter" connotes the political offspring, or the end-time nation being described.

Chapter 4

The Divine Appeal

The basic idea in prophecy is that of an omniscient God setting forth in human expression what will transpire in the future. And it is remarkably noteworthy how He so specifically calls attention to one matter of stupendous consequence.

Quoting from Jeremiah 50:45, we read: "Therefore hear ye the counsel of the LORD that he hath taken against Babylon." Of course, He does not here suggest we argue the matter, or advance our opinions, or evolve a spectacular thesis. No, He merely requests us to hear His counsel that He has taken against a certain Babylon, which, to all intents and purposes, appears to be an end-time nation, spiritually called Babylon. This council is prolifically stated in Jeremiah 50 and 51 and in Revelation 18. And, in hearing, it is exceedingly important to understand that the near and remote aspects of the Babylon doctrine are interspersed throughout Jeremiah 50 and 51, with both historical Babylon and prophetical Babylon in view.

It is conceded that one may not be able to distinguish between the fulfilled and the remote prophecies in some instances, but it would seem that a sufficient number can be definitely assembled in each category to make the investigation meaningful and satisfactory. As a Christian scholar of another day warned, we should never exchange a *verily* for an *if*. That is to say, if we can be certain about one reference and not so sure about another the unknown should not cause us to discard the known. And when it comes to the many references to Babylon in Jeremiah 50 and 51, a cursory glance will not produce the distinction between what is fulfilled and what is not. A novice may not detect the difference, but almost anyone, concentrating on the facts involved, will be rewarded with a degree of understanding.

In an Atlanta newspaper, I found the two following statements in separate advertisements:

"Delta Has 747 Flights to Los Angeles Daily"
"Eastern Has 3 Flights to Los Angeles Daily"

Imagine the reactions to these statements when viewed together, that is by those not conversant with flight parlance and not familiar with the kinds of planes in use. Not knowing that, in the first instance the number has to do with the type of craft, and in the second reference the number of trips, an uninformed person could think the former line was more popular, or had better service, or was faster. To the informed, there would be no problem of understanding. It is much the same in appreciating the message of the Bible.

This, of course, would be just as true in differentiating between the "day of Jacob's trouble" in the past and the "day of Jacob's trouble" that is yet to come as we find them in Jeremiah. The same would be true in distinguishing between the immediate plagues and the remote plagues of the Great Tribulation as found in the book of Joel. Both are there. Some fail to note this as well. On the other hand, many who do clearly see these particular distinctions have given little or no attention to distinguishing between historical Babylon and prophetical Babylon in Jeremiah 50 and 51. Both likewise are there.

The burden of this presentation is to isolate and to corre-late the prophetic elements of the remote kind in these Jeremiah contexts, to try to discover an entity, to learn what God says about the ultimate development and consequences.

Actually, when the prophet Jeremiah, by divine inspiration, says, "Hear ye the counsel of the LORD that he hath taken against Babylon," the emphasis is upon the fact that divine judgment is to fall on a certain Babylon. That is precisely what "counsel against" means. There seems to be a particular eagerness on the part of the speaker to get this point to register, and this point will be solemnly weighed later in this volume when we shall have gained, or attempted to have gained, some clearer appreciation of the entity in view.

Throughout the Bible, it is prominently revealed that divine communication is not too readily received by mankind. Earlier in the book of Jeremiah, the Most High God bent, as it were, over the parapet of heaven and asked pointedly, "To whom shall I speak?" (6:10). The prophet Isaiah urged, "Hear and your soul shall live." Jesus ended each of His seven epistles in the Apocalypse by saying, "He that hath an ear, let him hear what the Spirit saith unto the churches."

Thus, it is not a matter of eating forbidden fruit, or of intruding into restricted realms in attempting to discover what this particular judgment is going to be and upon whom it is to fall. We have God's own invitation to hear about it. And "to hear" suggests infinitely more than to lend an ear to an announcement. It means to hear one through on a given matter of importance — to get the facts clearly in perspective, to let them register indelibly, so the imparted communication may be understood and appreciated. Everyone, then, who ponders the matter at hand is responding to this divine appeal.

Divine Indignation Incurred

Neutrality has no place with Deity. He is either *with* or *against*.

Can antithesis be more striking? God speaks of being with His own, and of being against the wicked; that is, those who refuse to honor and obey His commands. Jesus said to His followers, "Go . . . and, Lo, I am with you." Jehovah said, "I am against thee, O Gog, the chief prince of Meshech and Tubal" (Ezek. 38:3). And the general consensus is that Russia is here being addressed. "Meshech" is thought to mean Moscow, and "Tubal" Tobolsk.

Now our attention is turned to the case of the "great city" and the devastating judgment which so suddenly and so disastrously will befall it.

It is solemn indeed when the God of love must express utter contempt, such as, "Behold, I am against thee, O thou most proud, saith the Lord . . . I will visit thee" (Jer. 50:31). "Visit thee" means in judgment. This bespeaks the end of divine patience and blessing, and prophetical Babylon, or the great city, incurs the indignation of Deity. Whatever the nation in view, and it is a particular nation as we shall later show, it is in trouble with the Most High God. No such nation, regardless of its vaunted strength, can protect itself if divine judgment is turned against it.

All nations sooner or later will be judged, for God has said, "I make a full end of all nations" (Jer. 30:11). This, of course, refers to the end of their sovereign position and self-government. But one prominent, powerful, once God-blessed Gentile nation is especially singled out for devastating annihilation prior to the divine judgment of all others, and this particular nation is spiritually called Babylon.

That company of believers who have an assured, safe, justified standing with the high court of heaven give little thought to the meaning of divine indignation, and those careless spiritually unconcerned people seldom entertain the possibility of such, but the indignation of God is the dreadful effect of His anger. But will He express it? Sir Winston Churchill, during

World War II, was asked, "Why are we fighting Hitler?" His reply was, "Let us stop and we'll find out." If it be asked, Why should we believe biblical predictions, the simple answer is, If we don't, we'll find out — the hard way.

The day of divine wrath against this earth is already scheduled, and may be in the not-too-distant future. It is called "the great tribulation," and because of its intensity and far-reaching sorrows, it is said to be without equal. Here is one scriptural comment on it:

> Come near, ye nations, to hear; and hearken, ye people: let the earth hear, and all that is therein; the world, and all things that come forth of it. For the indignation of the LORD is upon all nations, and his fury upon all their armies: he hath utterly [as of a future date] destroyed them, he hath delivered them to the slaughter.
>
> — Isaiah 34:1–2

During this prophesied period of outpouring judgment on this earth which has received without gratitude all the lavish divine blessings, and have denied God's sovereign claims, and have rebelled against His holy standards, the Lord will say to those Jews who accept Him as their Messiah, "Come, my people, enter thou into thy chambers, and shut thy doors about thee: hide thyself as it were for a little moment, until the indignation be overpast" (Isa. 26:20). Like a devastating tornado passing but leaving wanton destruction in its train, just so the indignation of the Lord will pass, but the horrendous results will be imponderable.

Regarding the destruction of prophetical Babylon, an end-time nation, here is a striking entry in the prophetic record: "The LORD hath opened his armoury, and hath brought forth the weapons of his indignation" (Jer. 50:25).

The words "hath opened" have a terrifying connotation.

They do not mean to draw upon a storehouse or stockpile of death-dealing agents, but to throw widely asunder, as the bursting dikes let go the immeasurable floods. And the expression, "weapons of his indignation," speaks of God's severest expression of wrath. This is not the empty palaver of a boulevard prognosticator; it is the promise of Him whose word cannot be broken. It will come to pass.

Just prior to this outburst of dreadful judgment, there will be a marvelous manifestation of divine mercy which "falleth as the gentle rain from heaven." It is a call for a modern exodus of Jews from the nation that is to be destroyed. Here is the record: "And I heard another voice from heaven, saying, Come out of her, my people, that ye be not partakers of her sins, and that ye receive not of her plagues [judgments]" (Rev. 18:4).

Is this a call for the church? No. A challenge for present-day believers? No. Of course, the Lord calls upon His people in every age to separate from all deception and confusion, from all that is contrary to His holy standards, but the church, the members of the body of Christ, are not in view here. They will have been caught up by this time to be with the Lord, evacuated from the scene before judgment falls (1 Thess. 4:16). "My people" is definitely an affectionate reference which Jehovah employed throughout the Old Testament when speaking of His covenant people, the Jews. So, just as the church is taken up into heaven to escape the Great Tribulation judgment, even so the Jews, especially the believing Jews, will be called out of the nation scheduled for judgment. Here is one reference to it: "Flee out of the midst of Babylon [an end-time nation], and deliver every man his soul: be not cut off in her iniquity; for this is the time of the LORD's vengeance; he will render unto her a recompence" (Jer. 51:6).

The church had a definite beginning. It will run its course to a scheduled conclusion. It will be taken to be with the Lord.

With its going, there will not be a true believer in the Lord and His way on the earth. But, since it is divinely decreed that the Word of Life shall be made available to all generations, one hundred forty-four thousand Jewish preachers will be ordained and sent forth (Rev. 7:4). Conceivably, one of their strongly-emphasized pleas will be, "Get thee out of the nation [spiritually] called Babylon, which the Lord is going to destroy." This could be one of the methods or means of getting the Jews back into the land of Israel.

And should the end-time nation in view be the U.S.A., then it would mean that God will evacuate the Jews (at least those who believe) out of it even as He took righteous Lot out of Sodom before His judgment came upon that city in the days of old. But whatever nation it may prove to be, out of it God will call all those who are His by faith in His salvation.

Those who will pack up and leave and go to Israel will have a striking testimony. We read, "The voice of them that flee and escape out of the land of Babylon, to declare in Zion the vengeance of the LORD our God" (Jer. 50:28).

Chapter 5

The Woman and the City

As the genuine has its counterfeit, so the true church has its imposter, composed of those who for the most part are of the highest ethical and moral persuasion, well-meaning and even devout. However, it should be evident to the thinking person that, as high principles alone could not take men to the moon, neither will admirable qualities in themselves take people to heaven. Certain spiritual conditions must be met. The Bible speaks of a narrow way which leads to life and a broad way which leads to destruction — a disillusionment of eternal proportions. We are all making our choice.

The Bible puts it another way. The tares will grow up with the wheat. At a predesigned time in the divine economy, the wheat will be gathered into the blissful abode, while the tares will be burned (eliminated). This elimination is termed the judgment of religious Babylon in Revelation 17, and Babylon here is referred to as an indecent woman. Then Revelation 18 records the judgment of political Babylon, which is designated "the great city."

In this whole account, there is one entry which occasions untold confusion in the minds of many. It is this: "The woman which thou sawest is that great city" (Rev. 17:18). At first sight, it would seem that the *woman* is the *city*. But there should be no real difficulty in understanding this comment if we properly regard the tense of the verb, the position of the verse in the context, and the usual symbolism of Scripture.

The verb is in the past tense. It tells of something already accomplished. It reveals that the Judge of all men has dealt with the *woman,* the false church, before ever turning to the judgment of the *city,* the political entity of the next chapter. Thus, the position of the statement, "The woman which thou sawest is that great city," is in a context entirely separate from the related facts pertaining to the city.

And as for the typical language employed, we should ask a few questions. For instance, can seven swine be seven years? Can seven ears of corn be seven years in the calendar? Can the bread which Jesus held in His hand at the Last Supper actually be His body? Can seven heads be seven mountains? Can ten horns be ten kings? Then may the woman be the city?

Let it be stated with the utmost simplicity that, whatever the answer is to the above questions, the same will be accurately true of this: Can the woman be the city? Yet many maintain that the Babylon of Revelation 17 is the same as the Babylon of Revelation 18. That is, they believe the woman is the city. This might be construed as an evasive attitude. It certainly is not a satisfactory resolution of an important prophetic matter.

There seems to be no expression in the Hebrew or the Greek languages comparable with the English words "symbolize," "typify," or "denote." When Joseph interpreted Pharaoh's dream of seven lean and seven fat swine and seven full ears of corn, he conveyed to him that fact that the lean swine and the lean ears of corn pointed to seven years of scarcity or famine, while the fat swine and full ears of corn meant seven years of prosperity. We have no problem understanding this symbolic language. No further question needs to be raised here.

The apostle Paul tells us that Jesus took the bread. "When he had given thanks, he brake it, and said, Take, eat: this is my body, which is broken for you" (1 Cor. 11:24). Some of our fine friends and relatives believe with a passionate fervor that the bread *is* Christ's body. They do not believe the swine and ears were actual years in the calendar, but they believe the bread *is* the body of Christ. Yet it is precisely the same grammatical expression as in the other references. But, note well the text — *He* took the bread. Did Jesus take His own body in His hand? It was He who broke the bread. He Himself was the agent in the operation. Did He break His own body?

When some get to Revelation 17, they become confused with the same grammatical construction and imagine all sorts of things, and evoke varying conclusions. They read, "The seven heads are seven mountains." Are they? No, they symbolize seven mountains, and the word, "mountain" symbolizes an empire or a nation. It is a political situation, not a geographical position. They are not seven hills on which Rome sits, but seven heads of state over which Rome has influence.

Now, perhaps we are prepared to take another look at the *woman.* "And the woman which thou sawest is that great city." That we have identically the same grammatical construction here as noted above is crystal clear.

Let us observe once again that the verb is in the past tense — "which thou sawest." While verbs at times may be a source of trouble in dealing with prophetical matters, since there is no time element with the eternal God who speaks about the future as though it were in the past, there is no problem here. The woman is said to have expired in Revelation 17:16. She has ended her career. She is gone from the scene. Completely disposed of, the woman cannot possibly be anything henceforth. It is a thorough elimination. Smoke will ascend from the plain of Shinar forever as a memorial to her destruction (Rev. 19:3). Here is the record:

And the ten horns which thou sawest upon the beast [the
ten kings under the control of the world dictator], these shall
hate the whore [religious Babylon], and shall make her desolate [non-operative] and naked [stripping her of all privi-
lege], and shall eat her flesh [expropriate her vast resourc-
es], and burn her with fire [eliminate utterly].

— Revelation 17:16

So the woman, which is religious Babylon, is no more, and the
symbolical terminology of Revelation 17:18, consistent with
the other similar constructions mentioned earlier, would mean,
"The woman which you saw in your vision symbolizes the great
city." That is to say, as went the woman, so shall go the city.
The Lord was telling John in this apocalyptic vision, "As I have
put an end to religious Babylon as a functioning entity, so shall
I destroy political Babylon."

Note well, the destruction of Babylon in Revelation 18:10
is the same as that in Jeremiah 50:46 from which it is quoted.
If the Revelation prophecy is not yet fulfilled, neither is the
Jeremiah prophecy. It is yet future.

It has been rightly said that the patience of God is the
greatest mystery of the hour. Man was created for the glory of
the Creator. It is therefore the whole duty of man to love God
and to glorify Him. Yet, with eyes too pure to behold evil, the
infinite God must look down upon gross and increasing wickedness, with murder, immorality, thievery, drunkenness, and
dope addiction ascending as a stench in His nostrils. Humankind, with persistent rebellion, little knows, and for the most
part cares less, that divine patience does have a point of cessation. Then judgment is inevitable. Justice demands it.

Blending Colors

We must now set ourselves to the task of discovering and ex-
amining the descriptions of political Babylon upon which the
indignation of the Lord is to be poured with limitless mea-

sure. Nor shall we want for material. The Spirit of God goes to almost unprecedented pains in describing the nation against which He has taken counsel, which counsel He requests us to hear.

A description is a word picture. Like the human artist who applies color after color and executes stroke upon stroke before an image becomes discernible, even so the divine Revealer splashes on the canvas of Scripture words that sparkle with vividness and multiply with frequency. Soon the fundamental image appears with clarity and convincing force. And, as it requires all the colors and all the strokes of the artist to make the picture, even so it necessitates all the descriptives to give us the fundamental image of the nation, spiritually called Babylon, against which the Lord has taken counsel.

There is a striking resemblance between the recorded characteristics of prophetical Babylon and the U.S.A. This will be generally agreed. Some characteristics, however are more convincing than others. Some are more tenable than others. In the end, they may only strike the reader as an analogy; but, taken as a whole, the consideration is extremely thought-provoking, and conceivably, when all the mysteries are unfolded, could prove the U.S.A. to be the very national entity God has in mind.

In such a consideration as this, we are handicapped by prejudice. It is ever distasteful to relate defeat or disaster to oneself, to one's family or to one's nation. Were some foreign national entity in view, say Russia or Cuba, we may not be too strongly predisposed toward sympathy.

Hosea prophesied that "Ephraim shall bring forth his children to the murderer" (9:13), and "Samaria shall become desolate; . . . they shall fall by the sword: their infants shall be dashed in pieces, and their women with child shall be ripped up" (13:16). At once the population dubbed him "a fool" and a "mad man" (9:7).

Malachi told the people of his day that God would tear down what they had built in their wickedness (1:4). He told them divine indignation would come upon them (1:4). They quickly reacted in a self-justifying manner: "Wherein have we polluted thee?" they insisted. And there was no change in their conduct. They simply did not believe God meant them.

Ezekiel in his faithful witness said, "Therefore thus saith the Lord GOD; I will also stretch out mine hand upon Edom, and will cut off man and beast from it; and I will make it desolate" (Ezek. 25:13). The people tore at him as thorns and briars.

We would be well advised to consider in their entirety the descriptions of the nation against which the Lord takes counsel, a nation which is spiritually called Babylon, a nation which will be sorely judged. The brushfuls He applies to the portrayal are vivid and dramatic, and blend into a perceptibly revealing picture.

Once the list of descriptions is set before us, we can attempt to find a nation to whom they are fittingly applicable either in ancient or contemporary times. They have to fit some nation.

Chapter 6

The Description of a Nation

Bible prophecy is not a sanctified astrology chart. We are not instructed to study the stars, but we are commanded to search the Scriptures. When we read that the Creator spoke worlds into being, we are forced to admit to the transcendence of His Word above His works.

How true and expressive are the words of the poet concerning the rhododendron:

> Tell them dear, if eyes were made for seeing,
> then beauty is its own excuse for being.

Poet, penman, and preacher alike have exulted with expletives aplenty in revealing about the beauty of the earth. And well they may, for the Creator expressed Himself as pleased. But since the Creator is greater than the thing created, then His Word is greater than His works. The Word of God is the transcript of His thoughts.

And no part of this divine transcript is more intriguing than the prophetic projection which comprises more than one-half of the whole Bible. It is called pre-written history. It is the facts of the future revealed today. Tennyson, in his *Locksley Hall,* said:

For I dipped into the future far as human eye could see;
saw the wonders of the world, and the glories that should be.

However, he confessed that his discerning expertise extended only as "far as human eye could see." Prophecy takes us far beyond all that men could dream.

Now we are ready to make an eschatological expedition. We will be prospecting for clues that can be fitted together, like the pieces of a jigsaw puzzle to give us a picture of an ethnic entity and its future. And again, we remind ourselves that persons, places, and things can be identified by description.

Babylon's Mother

Of all the multiplicity of descriptives which the Bible furnishes to characterize the particular nation which spiritually is called Babylon, none seems more logical with which to commence than this: "Your mother shall be sore confounded" (Jer. 50:12).

In what sense could historical Babylon have a mother? The city began with a man by the name of Nimrod. In what sense could Babylon the empire have a mother? It came into the ascendancy of Gentile dominion by divine authority when God interrupted His national dealings with Israel. In what sense could Babylon the city have a mother? Any reputable encyclopedia will reveal that Babylon, the capital of Babylonia, situated on the Euphrates, was one of the largest and most splendid cities of the ancient world, some sixteen hundred years before the Christian era. It was almost entirely destroyed in 683 B.C. A new city was built by Nebuchadnezzar nearly a century later. This city was taken by Cyrus in 538 B.C. and Babylonia became a Persian province at the time of Alexander the Great. The famous city fast declined. The original city was called Shinar by the Hebrews. The contemporary city is on the plains of Shinar in Hillah, some seventy miles south of Baghdad. It is clear that the Jeremiah prophecy of Babylon does not have these cities in view when speaking about the "mother of Babylon."

But the Scriptures state that prophetical Babylon has a mother. This "mother-nation" is in existence, though in a deteriorating condition, when daughter Babylon rises to the apex of her glory and incurs the indignation of God. The Bible says the mother-nation will be "sore confounded." Since this deleterious national condition is concurrent with the full development of the prophesied "daughter," we surely could not imagine the sorely confounded "mother" to be ancient Babylon. It is, rather, a kingdom from which this prophesied nation, spiritually called Babylon, has sprung, and is contemporary with it.

Should the U.S.A. be the end-time nation in view in this prophecy, then Britain, by the simplest deduction, would be the mother. And observe, please, Britain is at this hour precisely in the condition mentioned — sore confounded. The word "confounded" means "to pale," "to become dry" (in the vernacular, to dry up, shrink, or shrivel), "to lose strength."

On January 16, 1968, United Press International released an article in the news under the caption "The Nightfall of an Empire." It stated in part, "Britain yesterday abandoned her role as a world power. British Prime Minister Wilson's announcement before the House of Commons came after more than thirty-one hours of agonizing soul-searching by the British Cabinet."

No longer can the British proudly sing, "Britannia rules the waves," or say with patriotic fervor, "The sun never sets on her possessions." Britain is pale. She is shrinking. Her problems are almost insuperable, her future not too bright.

The daughter-nation naturally speaks the mother's language, perpetuates her culture and customs, and maintains a close relationship. This, of course, is what the U.S.A. has done with regard to Britain and, linguistically, more so than Canada which has two official languages.

Cup of Gold

"Babylon hath been a golden cup in the LORD's hand" (Jer. 51:7). The implications in this verse are many. The "golden cup" is in no sense a chalice (as is true with the woman or false church in Revelation 17:4). It is, rather, the thought of a cup of gold, negotiable worth, a means of exchange. We will see later that this prophesied nation, spiritually called Babylon, is a country that has been exceptionally blessed of God.

The idea concerning the "cup" is not only that of a container, but that from which the contents can be poured. The occurrences of the Word in the Scriptures are very numerous. Here are some examples:

The cup of salvation — Psalm 116:13
The cup of fury — Isaiah 51:17
The cup of trembling — Isaiah 51:22
The cup of consolation — Jeremiah 16:7
The cup of astonishment — Ezekiel 23:33
The cup of sorrow — Matthew 20:22
The cup of remembrance — Matthew 26:27
The cup of blessing — 1 Corinthians 10:16
The cup of devils — 1 Corinthians 10:21
The cup of the Lord — 1 Corinthians 11:27
The cup of indignation — Revelation 14:10
The cup of fierceness — Revelation 16:19

These references cover a wide area and touch upon various and diversified matters, but the cup of gold in the hand of the Lord commands our attention. The vessel in this instance is not wood, stone, or metal substance shaped by some skillful artificer into a utilitarian or ornamental arrangement. It is, rather, a great, God-blessed nation of unprecedented wealth in the whole of mankind.

And observe carefully where this "cup of gold" once was. It was in the hand of the Lord, that is to say, for His use. And what precisely does God do with gold? We are told He utilizes it to pave streets in the glorious city which one day will come down out of heaven and hover above the earth in space, and which will be the blissful home of Christians (Rev. 21). But what does Deity do with gold today in this earthly sphere?

For that matter, what precisely is God currently doing in the human realm? He is not now running governments, promoting industry, regulating commerce, or controlling finance. This is man's day. God is doing but one thing today. He is calling out a people for His name (Acts 15:14), and needs money to accomplish this. True, He owns all the gold as well as the cattle on a thousand hills, but He entrusts negotiable worth with man. Dedicated people give of their means that the Gospel may have a universal hearing.

No other nation has rivaled the U.S.A. in sending money and Bibles and missionaries to the ends of the earth. She has indeed been a monetary instrument of Deity in mission endeavor, but a rather alarming connotation attaches itself to the past tense of the verb — "hath been." The implication is that of a changed condition, which condition is of an adverse nature.

The true significance of the past tense in the statement, "Babylon hath been a golden cup in the Lord's hand," inheres in the fact, if our premise is sufficiently established, that the church will have been raptured — taken up to be with the Lord.

Since missionary money is given almost exclusively by those who will be taken, the nation in view will no longer be the source of such contributions; no longer a cup of gold in the hand of the Lord. And let us be reminded that approximately eighty-five percent of worldwide missionary support currently is from the U.S.A.

Where in either sacred or profane history is there any notice of Babylon the empire or Babylon the city pouring money into missionary endeavor? Babylon hindered rather than helped the people of God. It was Babylon which overran the Holy Land and raped it of its treasures. It was Babylon that sadistically gouged out the eyes of Zedekiah, the last king of Judah, but not until they had killed his sons in cold blood before him (Jer. 52:9–10). It was Babylon that caused the Jewish refugees to sit along its rivers and weep (Ps. 137:1). This was, rather, "death in the pot" (2 Kings 4:40) for God's people and not "gold in the cup" for His cause. There must be some other Babylon in view, or some other nation or kingdom spiritually called Babylon which fulfills the implications of the statement made.

Cosmopolitan Country

"A sword is upon . . . the mingled people that are in the midst of her" (Jer. 50:37), saith the Lord as He continues to reveal to us the counsel He has taken against a certain prophetical entity.

The nation in view consists of a "mingled people," and is, therefore, cosmopolitan in character. Here we must face the fact that, while this is a striking characteristic of the U.S.A., it could be applicable to other nations as well. However, just because a color has been used in another painting does not mean it does not find appropriateness in the one being developed. This "mingled people" contribution to the description is an important one.

The word "mingled" in the Hebrew simply means, "mixture" or "mongrel." Mongrel is defined as conveying the thoughts of mixed parentage, mixed origins, or formed of elements from different languages. This is certainly true of the U.S.A. Are we not one from many? Do we not have on our coins *"E pluribus unum"*? We have all come from some other country, directly or indirectly. Our country is often called the "melting pot."

The word "mingled" carries not only the thought of variety and diversity but strongly connotes integration or assimilation of these varying components into a cooperating and functioning whole. And the one, almost singular factor which makes this description more applicable to the U.S.A. than to any other country is the unilingual aspect. Other countries said to be a "mingled people" usually reflect it in a multilingual manner. Even our close neighbor, Canada, has two official languages. There is but one official language in the United States, and aliens seeking citizenship are required to speak it. The legal requirement reads, "Applicant must demonstrate an understanding of the English."

More and more our attention is being directed in the area of civil rights. We are reminded that all citizens in this mingled population should enjoy equally the privileges and opportunities of the land regardless of color, race, creed, or national origin. Indeed, minority groups are currently pressing for a fuller enjoyment of these rights which our Founding Fathers decreed they should have as citizens.

At any rate, the nation which God is describing is one particular nation. It is one that is cosmopolitan; and, while the term "mingled people" could apply, though with lesser force, to other nations, it must be allowed to register its full contribution to the picture before us. In the end, the consummation will furnish the proper perspective.

The Youngest Nation

"Behold, the hindermost of the nations shall be a wilderness, a dry land, and a desert" (Jer. 50:12).

Without doubt, this is the most poignant reference we have met thus far. It is a striking clue, for "hindermost" denotes the latest or most recent of the nations, the youngest of them all. Most nations were hoary with age when our country was born. As of this writing (1968) it is only one hundred ninety-two years since the U.S.A. was constituted as a sovereign state.

We have made fantastic strides in the development of our economy, and momentous advancements scientifically. We have lived so fast and so lavishly that our history books are more like fairy tales than facts. It seems but a brief moment from the creeping stagecoach to the supersonic jet; just an insignificant span from the Plymouth Rock hardships to contemporary comforts; just a fleeting shift of the shadow on the sundial from the slate and chalk to electronic computing techniques. The gristmill of vision, patriotism, determination, and untiring effort, plus the blessing of Almighty God, has ground out a huge amount of cherished history in an almost minute segment of time. We have risen to an enviable eminence among the countries of the earth.

This phenomenal development is not without explanation, and the explanation sparkles with the vision, courage, and dauntlessness on the part of those who, through blood and tears and prayers, fashioned, under God, the greatest and most glorious nation of all time out of a mingled people. They blended cultures and colors of varying and diverse kinds into a common commodity which we proudly call Americanism. We work and worship together. We play side by side; don the same uniform; carry the same flag. Dissident elements like ravaging disease germs in the human system, have plagued the body politic, but the "mingled people" have correlated and synchronized their loyalty, industry, and means to make their country and its economy excel all others on the face of the earth.

But, this ethnic infant of which God speaks, like a spoiled child which has been lavished with gifts, is going to be spanked.

The Word of the Lord has declared it! It "shall be a wilderness, a dry land, and a desert" (Jer. 50:12). Even though it is couched in figurative expression, every thinking individual who hears this counsel as God requested, would understand that this declaration is weighted with a terrifying outcome.

To what Babylon of history could this description possibly apply? The Babylonian Empire was subdued by the Medes and Persians, but it did not become a desert. The "hindermost" qualification would obviate conclusively the idea of antiquity.

A Nation of Wealth

Another brush full goes on the canvas. The colors are multiplying. The prophet now applies this: "O thou that dwellest upon many waters, abundant in treasures, thine end is come, and the measure of thy covetousness" (Jer. 51:13).

Here we have two words, "abundant" and "treasures," pregnant with meaning, each of which suggests rich connotations. "Abundant" is primarily a Bible word. That is, it is more appropriately oriented in scriptural composition. The definitive illustration is that of putting a vessel under a running faucet. The water rises, reaches the brim, then runs over, or abounds. The U.S.A. has "abounded" generously toward many of the underprivileged nations in food and medical supplies and financial aid.

The word "treasures" does not refer to valuable commodities, but to the storehouse containing them. It is the Hebrew word *o-tsawr*, meaning a depository, an armory, a granary, etc. It is derived from the word *aw-tsar*, which means to store, to lay up. It adds up to a fabulous amassing of fortunes, and indicates that the nation about which God is speaking is the wealthiest of all. This conclusion becomes, seemingly, irrefutably established with subsequent characteristics to be noted.

In this connection, we are reminded that the U.S.A., comprising only seven percent of the world's population, is in possession of more than half of the world's wealth. She has sixty-three percent of the world's manufactured goods, seventy-four percent of the world's automobiles, fifty-two percent of the world's trucks, fifty-six percent of the world's telephones, forty-seven percent of the world's radios, forty-six percent of the world's electric output, fifty-two percent of the world's steel, fifty-three percent of the world's petroleum, and consumes thirty-five percent of the world's energy.

Our gross national product and income rose from $284,769,000,000 in 1950, to $743,288,000,000 in 1966, and to $939,161,000,000 in 1972. This is astronomical — singular in the history of nations.

These are fantastic statistics, but they are fraught with an ever-existing danger. In the divine economy is a rigid rule of responsibility — "For unto whomsoever much is given, of him shall be much required" (Luke 12:48). If this is spoken primarily of an individual, let it be remembered that individuals make up nations, and God speaks of nations forgetting Him, and the serious consequences resulting from this neglect.

We are indeed a forgetful people! Seldom do we think about the price of our heritage. We are an ungrateful people. By and large, we are unmindful of the Bestower of our blessings. Then, too, we have become despicably self-sufficient. We have deified the intellect and exalted man. Revelling in our accomplishments, we are building our "tower of Babel" into the heavens. We are so egocentric we have parted company with the Most High God. We are so foolish as to think we can pick a path through the jungle of reason and come out satisfactorily. But not so. It is a course of inevitable failure.

Once the Hon. W. E. Gladstone viewed such a tendency in this way: "One thing frightens me. I am afraid God is dying out in the minds of men." This is the trend in our land today.

He who reveals this counsel about an end-time nation, spiritually called Babylon, unequivocally declares, "Thine end is come, and [together with] the measure of thy covetousness" (Jer. 51:13). Thus, it is a nation no longer worthy of divine blessing, one that has bartered away its privileges, and one that shall cease to exist.

Prestigiously Great

The picture is developing. Here is a vivid brush full: "How is the hammer of the whole earth cut asunder and broken! how is Babylon become a desolation among the nations! (Jer. 50:23). That is to say, Is it not unimaginable that a nation so wealthy and so powerful could be cut off and become an utter desolation?

Take a look at the word "hammer." The verb form means to formulate, to shape, or to create as if by hammer strokes; to force or drive as if by repeated blows; to overpower, to overwhelm, or to overrule by persistent force or influence.

Said W. Somerset Maugham, "I wondered if the poor devil had been hammered on the stock exchange."

Webster says, "to make reiterated effort."

The word "hammer," while connoting force or power, does not here indicate destructiveness. A hammer is not categorized as a weapon, but rather as a tool. The hammer of diplomacy can register telling blows when wielded by a great political power.

No descriptive word in the almost interminable delineation of characteristics is more highly figurative than this particular one. The word "hammer" has a wide application, so wide in fact that there could be as many applications suggested as the number of people applying them. This is one of the many reasons why care should be cautiously exercised and dogmatism restrained in dealing with such matters.

We must be reminded again and again, however, that it has pleased the divine Revelator to couch prophecy in strange but vivid language. The portrayal of the coming world dictator (Antichrist) may at times seem meaningless, even grotesque, such as seven heads and ten horns, but the symbolism sooner or later unfolds into understandable terms. The true meaning will always be obscured in description until sufficient elements combine to make the image unmistakably evident. God gave His Word to convey Truth, and such truth must become apparent or the divine purpose in giving it would be destroyed.

Getting back to the text, it is ever the insatiable desire of the leaders of great nations to use the hammer of influence in strong, far-reaching strokes. Governor Claude Kirk of Florida, representing American governors on a fact-finding mission to Europe regarding monetary difficulties, said, "I think we have to have seventy dollars per ounce of gold with the right of Americans to own it. . . . We are the No. 1 nation — we can create the rules" (Associated Press, May 3, 1968). It requires a strong nation to wield a hammer like that, or to suggest doing so. Imagine a small country like Syria, Lebanon, or Iran speaking in this manner.

Dr. Henry Kissinger, the U.S. Secretary of State, addressed the leaders of Britain at a dinner given in his honor. It was a stop on one of his "hurricane" schedules of hopscotching from one country to another seeking peace.

With Britain beleaguered by a work-stoppage, terrifying inflation, and the oil crisis, the Secretary of State gained some appreciable applause when he said that our nation, together with the NATO countries and Japan, would find sufficient technological know-how and united determination to rise out of the disturbing fuel crisis in spite of Arab embargoes against us. He assured them that the U.S. was prepared and ready to contribute impressive amounts of intellectual and monetary assistance to the project.

Dr. Kissinger has had no peer in his effective and amazing use of international diplomacy. He is received by world leaders whether friendly or unfriendly to our country. When an Arab diplomat was asked how an American Jew could wield any influence with the Arab nations, his terse reply was, "It is a modern miracle." He has the power of "the hammer" behind him.

As the omniscient God looked down through the corridors of time, He saw the nation, which He is here describing, as wielding the greatest influence of any country — "the hammer of the whole earth." The U.S.A. has unquestionably held that distinction.

Amazing Attainments

"Though Babylon should mount up to heaven . . . yet from me shall spoilers come unto her, saith the LORD" (Jer. 51:53). Regardless of prophetical Babylon's attainments, her wealth and prosperity, it will be observed how frequently God reiterates the inevitably disastrous end to be experienced.

Of the many meanings for the word "mount," three stand out prominently as having the most pertinence. They are *exalt, excel,* and *increase.* They would seem to present this thought: With enormous technological advances, with abounding natural resources, the increase of productivity and scientific breakthroughs, the nation, spiritually called Babylon, will excel all other countries in attaining an exalted position among the peoples of the earth. Russia may have the jump on the U.S.A. in one or two areas, but in the overall picture, our country far excels all others in accomplishments, in wealth, and in comfort.

The expression "mount up to heaven" not only has some hints of divine displeasure, but suggests a spiritual classification. Was it not Satan, the prince of this world, the instigator of Babylonism, who said, "I will ascend into heaven, I will exalt [myself]" (Isa. 14:13)? Was it not Nimrod, Satan's chief "advance man," who led his contemporaries in saying, "Let us build us a city and a tower, whose top may reach unto heaven; and let us make us a name" (Gen. 11:4)?

Then there is the literal application. Who ever dreamed a few short years ago that the U.S.A. would be spending vast sums of money in an attempt to explore outer space and to land men on the moon? Yet, by the miracle of television, most of us have clearly seen men walking on the moon. Russia has put men into outer space, but *only* the U.S.A. has "mounted up to heaven" or to a heavenly planet. One thing is certain, ancient Babylon never accomplished such a feat.

We should be reminded, however, that man was created for the earth and not for outer space. That is why, when man leaves the earth, he must take his atmosphere with him. Here are a few expressive verses in point:

"The heaven, even the heavens, are the LORD's: but the earth hath he given to the children of men" (Ps. 115:16).

"And hath made of one blood all nations of men for to dwell *on all the face of the earth,* and hath determined . . . the bounds of their habitation" (Acts 17:26 — emphasis added).

". . . Though they climb up to heaven, thence will I bring them down" (Amos 9:2).

God does not say that man shall not attain super-atmospheric goals, but when he does, he has jumped the divinely-set bounds, and God will bring him down. Just what this actually means is not clear, but it certainly bespeaks ultimate defeat instead of permanent success. Yet, for all of this, the matter of mounting up to heaven may be an overall characterization — an increasing, excelling, exalting condition which spawns pride, haughtiness, and forgetfulness of God. Imagination is not required to drape this description about the national attitude of our land.

Voice of Influence

The divine artist adds a deep color to the emerging portrait of the nation, spiritually called Babylon, when He says, "Because the LORD hath spoiled Babylon, and destroyed out of her the great voice; when her waves do roar like great waters, a noise of their voice is uttered" (Jer. 51:55).

It is a clear admission on the highest authority that the nation in view speaks with a great voice; that her pronouncements elicit wide attention; that her expressed suggestions can tip the balance in the direction of her wishes; that her voice is prestigiously regarded; that, alas! the day will come when that voice will be silenced, and that forever. As a bullet from an assassin's gun can still in a moment the voice of a great leader, even so the judgment from the hand of the Lord will end the voice of the great nation.

Instantaneous global communication and supersonic transportation, buttressed by wealth and power, have encouraged more and more a voice on the part of the U.S.A., not only in matters directly affecting its own interests, but in problems among others as well. We rush envoys to troubled areas to aid in effecting settlements, and usually take the credit when the solution is reached. And all of this may be perfectly sensible in a world which constantly grows smaller and in an era of interdependence. An illustration in point was the recent controversy between Turkey and Greece over Cyprus. Our "voice" was there.

Said U.S. Rep. Thomas L. Ashley, "America has a moral responsibility to maintain global involvement in the world's affairs" (*Toledo News,* April 28, 1968).

If the Bible quotation concerning "the great voice" should point up the U.S.A., let it be said with patriotic pride her voice has been for the most part one of honor; her commitments have been fulfilled even to the point of sacrificing her beloved sons on foreign soil. But her voice is meeting as never before with bullish opposition by Russia and her satellites which are slowly rendering it ineffective in international diplomacy. This was especially demonstrated in the Security Council's debate over the Israeli-Arab war of 1967. The whole world heard the rebuffs.

But the final articulation of the nation in view will not be that of a famous political power, that for so long sounded forth gloriously in the earth, swaying kings and kingdoms, with the hammering strokes of preponderant influence, but, sadly indeed, the roaring cries of a writhing, perishing people whose might will serve as no deterrent in the hour of doom and desolation. This is the inevitable end of the nation about which God has taken counsel.

Excellent Fortifications

Our generation is the first in history to concern itself so prominently about protection from possible enemy attacks. In recent years, the matter of bomb shelters has approached hysteria. Radio network alerts are tested intermittently, and highways all over the country have ominous signs reading, "Evacuation route." With our avowed enemies possessing devastating weapons in formidable quantities, the fear of attack is ever present, and our leaders have gone to unprecedented ends to establish what they hope will be impenetrable defense systems. The nation God is describing to us is notable for such an effort, but, evidently, to no avail. Here is a solemn entry.

> Though Babylon should mount up to heaven [in technological know-how and in scientific advancement], and though she *should fortify the height of her strength* [do all in her power for self-protection], yet from me shall spoilers come unto her, saith the LORD.
>
> —Jeremiah 51:53 — emphasis and remarks added

---

*Keep in mind this was written in the midst of the Cold War.

The word "fortify" means to make inaccessible by height, or restraint. Ancient Babylon had high walls, strong enough to withstand the bombarding of the battering rams and too high for the enemy to vault. Says the *Times Encyclopedia,* "Ancient Babylon was in the form of a square, each side fifteen miles long, with walls of such immense height and thickness as to constitute one of the wonders of the world."

The intimations of the above prophecy, however, go far beyond stone walls, for prophetical Babylon will be concerned, not about foot soldiers and battering rams, but about outer space attacks of hostile forces. Thus, she will "mount up to heaven" to the fullest extent of her ingenuity and to the ultimate of her resources. For instance, the Strategic Air Command with its intricate and extensive system would be an appropriate illustration, indeed a classic example.

The Strategic Air Command, headquartered at Offut Air Force Base, Nebraska, is the long-range bomber and missile force of the U.S. Air Force. Its combat-ready air forces can strike anywhere in the world. SAC includes 2nd, 8th, 15th, and 16th air forces. It has about thirteen hundred jet bombers and tanker airplanes. SAC uses several types of missiles, including intercontinental ballistic missiles.

SAC's communications network can mobilize the entire command within seconds after a warning. A bomber force can be on the way to its target within fifteen minutes after a warning. If an enemy attack were to destroy SAC's ground control centers, retaliatory attacks would be directed from an airborne command plane. One of these planes is in the air at all times.

For security reasons, there are not many facts and figures available. SAC is but one phase of many precautionary defense measures being developed by the U.S.A., thus reflecting the terrible threat of destructive war in our scientific age. How insufficient would be the protective measures of recent years. The Hindenburg line, erected by the Germans in 1916 during

World War I across northeastern France from Lille south through St. Gobain, and thence east to Rethel, later to Vouziers and Metz, was thought to be a strong line of defense.

The Hindenburg line and the Maginot wall today would be as useful as mosquito netting in containing an enraged lion in the face of the nuclear capability of our foes. Thus, as the text intimates concerning prophetical Babylon, our country "fortifies to the height of her strength." And so far as the United States is concerned, the word "strength" might be comprehended in this announcement: "The Nixon Administration has decided to ask Congress for almost $99 billion in new spending authority for defense, including $92.6 billion in the new budget and $5.9 billion in supplemental funds for last year" (*St. Petersburg Times,* January 20, 1974).

Perhaps a few additional facts on this subject might prove interesting. The *Nation's Business* (May 1968) asks, "How strong militarily must the United States be in the years ahead?" The Secretary of Defense quickly replied that he was for expanding the nuclear weapons and missile stockpiles, then added:

Our armed forces and men available for call-up total about 3.4 million. In the European theater, NATO forces are slightly under 960,000 Warsaw Pact troops. We have great mobility now. For example, when the fiscal year 1968 orders are delivered, we'll have 7,500 modern turbine helicopters. We now have considerable airlift capability to deploy troops quickly to any part of the globe. The Spartan will intercept enemy missiles at altitudes outside the atmosphere. The Sprint will climb thousands of feet in a few seconds, via a gas-pressured getaway technique, and stop objects several miles from target. A new airborne warning system will take care of enemy bombers. Over-the-horizon radars planned for bomber plane defense will also provide for missiles flung from submarines. A satellite-borne missile warning system is in the making.

Eric Burgess, in his book *Guided Weapons,* says:

> Rocket vehicles capable of vast destruction of military objectives continents away from the launching site are no longer a remote dream, but a present nightmare. Besides the awesome intercontinental ballistic missiles are the short-range and intermediate ones — the Polaris, Redstone, Viking, Nike, and many others. The air force has at its own command tactical missiles, strategic missiles, air-to-air missiles, air-to-ground missiles, and surface-to-air interceptors, with bombers capable of flying at great speed and height to deliver their thermonuclear weapons.

Anyone interested could readily find in the local library volumes of information on present-day sophisticated weapons that would stagger the intellect. Yet there is much in the way of modern devastating weaponry which the Defense Department understandably has not made known to the public. When the Scriptures tell about a nation that "fortifies to the height of her strength," one cannot help but think of the U.S.A., because no other nation has ever been known to, nor is now known to, do so much in the way of national security.

World Involvements

The counsel of the Lord against Babylon, as is biblically stated, is seen more and more in derogatory and denunciatory statements, such as, "O thou that dwellest upon many waters . . . thine end is come" (Jer. 51:13).

The idea conveyed by "dwellest," among other things, is "to set up" or "to establish oneself." The imagination could run widely afield here were it not for the accompanying word "waters." We must keep in mind we are dealing with prophecy, and in eschatology, as well as in other areas of divine Truth, if not more so, we should compare scripture with scripture.

Speaking of prophetical religious Babylon, John explained that an angel came to him and said, "Come hither; I will shew unto thee the judgment of the great whore [the composite of false religious organizations] that sitteth upon many waters" (Rev. 17:1). Then follows an elucidating statement: "The waters which thou sawest, where the whore sitteth [in Jeremiah "dwellest"], are peoples, and multitudes, and nations, and tongues" (Rev. 17:15).

The above text, Jeremiah 51:13, does not say "upon *all* waters," but rather on "many waters." The Babylon God has in view is an end-time nation which has in one way or another established herself in many countries.

In this connection, we are reminded that we have military bases, manufacturing plants, oil refineries, offices, etc., in many parts of the world. And, the literal meaning of waters need not be overlooked in this connection. We have warships, aircraft carriers, and naval installations on all the great bodies of water, to say nothing of submarines which ply their way through the seas and the oceans.

There are indeed many ways in which the U.S.A. has connections with many nations.

At present, the United States is committed to help defend forty-two nations on every continent except Africa under the eight post-World War II treaties. And in Africa, the U.S.A. is pledged to ponder what action it should take should Liberia be the victim of aggression. Saudi Arabia has a presidential pledge that its integrity will be protected.
—*Montebello News,* February 15, 1968

Such widespread involvements as these may point up the reason why so many nations will react mournfully when this prophesied nation comes to her end as is so clearly predicted.

"And the kings of the earth, who have committed fornication and lived deliciously with her, shall bewail her, and lament for her, when they shall see the smoke of her burning" (Rev. 18:9).

Apparently, the conquering force which deals the death-blow will release pictures taken by their reconnaissance planes in the aftermath of their triumph, for we read that the people of the earth "shall see the smoke of her burning" (Rev. 18:9).

Whatever the identity of the powerful, wealthy nation that falls, can one envision the TV viewing of this unprecedented catastrophe around the world — great cities ablaze as the national economy is hopelessly destroyed? Should it be the U.S.A., can one imagine such an indescribable holocaust?

We, of course, would hope that this shall not be the fate of our fair land, but, if we believe the Word of God, we must understand that this is precisely what is going to befall some nation. And that nation will answer to the descriptions the Lord has so thoroughly given in His prophetic declaration.

Foreign Aid

Here is an illuminating entry. "The merchants of the earth are waxed rich through the abundance of her delicacies" (Rev. 18:3).

The word "delicacies," which stands alone in New Testament Truth, permits almost exorbitant connotations. It is the thought of luxury plus voluptuousness. It is a condition which leads to an insensible kind of generosity, such as an inebriated person, with senses confused, wanting to treat everyone regardless of the number or the cost or his ability to foot the bill.

The above Bible text, of course, like the ten previous characteristics concerns a nation, and we do not need to overwork our imagination to find an apt illustration.

In an editorial under the caption "The Global Giveaway," the *Chicago Tribune*,* November 2, 1967, commented:

---

*Used by written permission.

Rep. Otto E. Passman (D. La.), chairman of the House appropriations subcommittee, has been advised that the net total of foreign aid through fiscal year 1967 is $114,694,000,000 dollars. Rep. Passman calculates the total cost of foreign aid since 1956, including interest the government paid on money borrowed to give away, as $152,533,000,000.

The editorial continues:

New grants and loans to foreign countries now exceed $6 billion a year, and the net total, after all interest and principal payments, is well over $5 billion. Thus, the total cost of foreign aid, including interest on the debt, is more than $10 billion a year. Rep. Passman charges that the foreign aid program has been "fragmentized" to confuse the people. He says the oil flows from sixteen different "spigots," and that each year Congress is asked in more than a dozen items of proposed legislation to increase the spending or lending authority of the dispensing agencies.

The editorial observes:

If the grant aid of $12,928,000,000 extended by the United States under the Marshall plan from 1949 through 1952, and $8,724,000,000 under the mutual act from 1953 through 1957 had consisted of interest-bearing security loans, the prosperous countries of Europe, as well as Japan, would be repaying us now, with interest, and there would be no balance on payments problem. Instead, these countries are accumulating huge gold and dollar reserves and exporting manufactured products at prices with which the United States cannot compete.

The Lord in the long ago revealed that the merchants of the earth would wax rich through the voluptuous luxury and great generosity of an end-time nation, spiritually called Babylon.

The term "waxed rich" indicates economic assistance to a marked degree, and "of the earth" speaks of the extensive outreach of such liberality. And it must be noted that there is no condemnation in the text because of the distribution of such wealth, for "the Lord loveth a cheerful giver." Yet, it is to be expected that, when characteristics are being cited, one of this exceptional type would naturally be prominent in the list. It is of course a chief identifying quality of the U.S.A.

Blatant Covetousness

The divine artist mixes two deep colors on His palette as He saturates the brush for this application to the picture which becomes more and more vivid: "It is the land of graven images, and they are mad upon their idols" (Jer. 50:38).

The verb form for the word "graven" means to shape, to evolve, to invent. Thus, the nation in view is a land of great inventions. The power to conceive and present new combinations of facts, or ideas, to devise new methods or instruments, encouraged by monetary means, natural resources, and favorable opportunity, has flourished in our young democracy. Ours is impressively a land of great inventions, bringing us to the point of a push button existence, loading us with benefits undreamed of heretofore. But, while we can computerize ourselves into amazing achievements, we are stalked with the grim specter of spiritual and moral deterioration.

The expression "mad upon their idols" points to the nation becoming idolatrous and obsessed with her lusts — a lethal kind of diabolical deception which eventuates in spiritual disinterest, disorientation, disunity, degeneration, decadence — disaster. Idolatry is rendered "covetousness" in Colossians 3:5, and covetousness means "wanting more" — the age-long propensity of man. This is reflected both in capital and in labor. Thus, there are strikes, boycotts, and athlete holdouts to force a gratification of such insatiable longings.

This condition is undebatably true in America. We live sumptuously but want more. One basketball player this year will receive a salary of two hundred fifty thousand dollars to do in a small part of the year what once was only a playful game. A twenty-four–year–old girl will get one hundred sixty-five thousand dollars this year for a few appearances on TV. Any number of baseball players will draw more than one hundred thousand dollars this year. One one-hour-a-week-for-nine-months TV program costs thirty-four million dollars to produce. Other such programs may exceed this figure. All the while, people are in want in our own land and many are starving in other parts of the world.

"Mad upon their idols" reveals an insane pressing for gratification of lusts, with such obsessions destroying all restraints and producing a moral and spiritual breakdown like unto Sodom and Gomorrah. In *Time* magazine (November 1967), Max Lerner is quoted as saying, "America is now living a Babylon existence."

Epicurean Traits

The color next applied seems to tint the whole portrait. "How much she hath glorified herself, and lived deliciously" (Rev. 18:7). This brush full makes a striking contribution to the desired perspective. It is a general characteristic, poignantly identifying.

"Hath glorified herself" refers to attitude, not to attainment; to personal conduct, not to profitable contribution. The emphasis, at least in God's sight, is comparable with that of historical Babylon, which said, "Let us make us a name" (Gen. 11:4). Prophetical Babylon will have distinguished herself in science, in industry, in commerce, in finance, and in art, but will have become woefully independent of God. This, by the very nature of things, even without intent or design, is tantamount to self-glorification, a self-sufficiency which can only eventuate in disillusionment.

Men may scoff at the suggestion, but as in Jeremiah's day, it is such a course of fleshly enjoyment and flamboyant indifference toward the infinite God which leads toward the precipice of disaster. The witness of history cannot be silenced. They would not believe God then (Jer. 6:10); we will not believe God now. Jehovah pleaded, "Turn ye, turn ye from your evil ways; for why will ye die?" (Ezek. 33:11). Further, "Amend your ways and your doings, and I will cause you to dwell in this place" (Jer. 7:3). And still further, "Repent, and turn yourselves from your idols; and turn away your faces from all your abominations" (Ezek. 14:6). The reaction of those ancient people was one of adamant indifference and persistent rebellion.

Take a look at the outcome. See the Israelites sitting by the rivers of Babylon, weeping, having been ejected from their land. See the pitiful five hundred thousand starving to death in Poland. See the six million tortured and killed under Hitler. There is no remorse so bitter, or tears of regret so hot, as the kind which could have been averted by man glorifying God rather than catering to himself.

The "living deliciously" aspect of this description should be an understandable one — a sensual, intemperate, gluttonous kind of habitual sublimation which subjugates all tenets of holy conduct and all rules of proper physical behavior to the unrestrained propensities of desire. This type of comportment flourishes in the climate of prosperity, more so than ever today. "I spake unto thee in thy prosperity; but thou saidst, I will not hear. This hath been thy manner from thy youth [the early days of Israel], that thou obeyedst not my voice" (Jer. 22:21).

An illustration in point, so far as our country is concerned, may be noted in the exorbitant tab we pick up each year: Americans spend annually

for food — $84,000,000,000;
for recreation — $21,500,000,000;
for illegal gambling — $47,000,000,000;
for alcoholic beverages — $11,000,000,000;
for tobacco — $8,000,000,000;
for pets — $3,500,000,000; and
for dog food — $210,000,000.

Said a TV reporter just returned from an Eastern assignment, "We spend millions for hand lotions and hair tonic while vast multitudes are hungry in India and many are starving." We live deliciously!

A delegate to the World Congress on Evangelism in Berlin made this public statement upon his return:

The Americans were readily distinguishable from the delegates of other nations in two respects. First, in their better dress. Second, in their desire to eat. At the close of the day, some Colombian delegates inquired, "Where is the nearest prayer room?" while the Americans invariably asked, "Where is the nearest restaurant?"

It is not an uncomely trait for people to be neatly and attractively attired. Nor is it unusual for people to experience an urge to eat. But we have moved an alarming distance from the devotion of holy Job who testified, "I have esteemed the words of his [God's] mouth more than my necessary food."

What the scriptural description reveals is that prosperity, pride, and God-rejection spawn an intemperance, an incontinence, even a moral ruthlessness, which bode ill for any society. It is an index into the human products of apostate times. These are indeed apostate times, and these are indeed the prevailing conditions. If we may resort to the vernacular, "America is living it up!"

Spiritual Decadence

Prosperity leads to self-sufficiency; self-sufficiency leads to spiritual decadence; spiritual decadence leads to moral corruption. Such spiraling incontinence sooner or later reaches heaven; that is, it mounts so alarmingly that it calls down the indictment of Deity. And here is the divine complaint about the end-time nation which is called Babylon: "Her sins have reached unto heaven" (Rev. 18:5).

In a related commentary, this entry should be noted: "She hath been proud against the LORD, against the holy one of Israel" (Jer. 50:29). Even the appellation used for Deity in this reference inferentially is condemning. When God speaks of His being the "holy one," He intimates that the people are unholy.

That which is against the Lord is sin. Any unrighteousness is sin, and pride in unholy conduct is the forerunner of all indignities against the Most High. It may be under the guise of new morality or situational ethics, but if it is contrary to the divine standards, it is categorically condemned as sin. Sin is not only "a reproach to any people," it is an offense to the Lord.

In a worldwide broadcast recently, the speaker, quoting from a prominent publication, said, "Morals dipped more last year than in the fifty previous years." He was referring to the U.S.A. It could well be that God was speaking of the same nation. Sordid statistics may only soil the mind, and daily exhibits are everywhere in evidence, but the following may serve as something of an index into our crumbling foundations or morality:

U.S. crime is said to be growing five times faster than our population — juvenile crime seven times faster. Arrests of persons under eighteen have increased ten percent each year during the past five years. In ten years illegitimate births have increased three hundred percent, and venereal disease has increased seventy-two percent in one year. The sale of obscene materials (mostly to children) is a multi-million-dollar-a-year business. Prison population is at an all-time peak. Our crime bill is twenty billion dollars per year. There are said to be nine and a half million confirmed alcoholics and an estimated ten million problem drinkers. Combine all our churches, synagogues, and temples, and they are outnumbered by our taverns by one hundred seventy-five thousand.

A San Francisco newspaper article, with an accompanying photograph, gave this account:

> The topless craze stole from the flattering gloom of North Beach nightclubs into a pitiless noonday glare on Broadway yesterday. The girls who paraded with bare bosoms in front of the Peppermint Tree were more studies in sheer business brassiness than devilish allurement for the neighborhood fleshpots. The excuse for it all was an alleged labor dispute involving the management of the Peppermint Tree and "professional" topless dancers who say they have been aced out of their jobs by zealous "amateurs." The complaint is that fourteen professionals earning about one hundred fifty dollars a week were fired two weeks ago to make way for the amazing number of women who are prepared to dance stripped to the waist — for free.

United Press International (January 20, 1974) reported a growing sex craze, "encounter" parlors where men pay one dollar a minute to talk to naked ladies. The parlors have names like the House of Ecstasy, Cupid's Corner, the Tunnel of Love, the House of Joy, Brandy's, the Powell Nude Encounter Parlor, Naked City, and Den of Love, and for one dollar a minute a nude hostess will sit and talk or read a dirty book to customers who enter the storefront operations.

When a thrice-holy God states that "her sins have reached

unto heaven," it is an intimation that His longsuffering is being taxed to the breaking point. And when He adds, "She hath been proud against the LORD," He is indicating the brazenness and boldness with which such sinning is committed before His all-seeing eyes. It is a critical condition, one that can but lead to inevitable judgment, and this is precisely what is predicted for an end-time nation, spiritually called Babylon.

Egotistically Blind

As the skill of an artist produces the finer details of a subject, even so the omniscient Discerner of hearts can translate into verbal expression what humans entertain in their thoughts. It was said of Jesus that "he knew what was in man." God knows what is in their minds (John 2:25). Here is one of the finer but more important details in depicting prophetical Babylon: "For she saith in her heart, I sit a queen . . . and shall see no sorrow" (Rev. 18:7).

Unlike Hiroshima, Berlin, London, North Vietnam, and other unfortunate places, America has never felt the sting of devastating bombs.* We sit a queen! We are the greatest! We are the most powerful! We are the best! Are not these expressive of the general attitude and the vocal declaration? "It can't happen here" (which seems to be the prevailing thought) is tantamount to the textual expression, "shall see no sorrow." Well, let us not be too sure. Israel had to learn the hard way. Judah likewise. No nation that forgets God can long prosper. Jerusalem, the holy city, went down under the devastating attack of Titus in A.D. 70, a complete shambles.

An apostate atmosphere has an acute tendency to dim spiritual vision. Few will take God's pronouncements at face value, but they are always proved to be true. Paul, in that horri-

---

*This statement was true until the bombing of the Alfred P. Murrah Federal Building in Oklahoma City on April 19, 1995.

fying Mediterranean storm, when neither sun nor moon nor stars was visible for a fortnight, stood amid the two hundred eighty-five sailors on the floundering ship and declared, "Sirs, be of good cheer: for I believe God, that it shall be even as it was told me" (Acts 27:25).

Our foresight is suffering decline rapidly. We ought to know that a society cannot long exist with home life disintegrating, church influence declining, and legislative principles departing. Centralized power, corruption in politics, lawlessness in the streets, deficit spending, loss of ideals, disregard for life — these and many other conditions are destroying the fabric of our national life. Yet, we all hope for the best while we espouse the worst. More and more the U.S.A. is assuming a revolutionary posture, but not for good.

One recently warned, "Our nation is on the skids, at the base of which descent all other nations, taking the same course, have come to disaster." Yet we accelerate our speed in such a course rather than reverse our trends. We "sit a queen . . . and shall see no sorrow." And so it goes in modern America where the dauntless spiritual devotion of Plymouth Rock has given way to a daring departure from all that is high and holy.

The symptoms of decay have been rapidly developing in our young nation. After the assassination of Senator Robert Kennedy, many were the voices diagnosing our fair land as a "sick nation." The president and others tried hard to play down this disturbing inference, but our country is sick. Sin makes any nation sick. Our symptoms are analogous with Israel's, and the Great Physician made this entry in His Record: ". . . the whole head is sick, and the whole heart faint. From the sole of the foot even unto the head there is no soundness in it; but wounds, and bruises, and putrifying sores" (Isa. 1:5–6).

Dr. John B. Streator, pastor of the First Baptist Church in San Francisco, and formerly a missionary in China, writes:

The first time I came in contact with student demonstrations was when I first went out to China in 1947. I remember at the time the reaction was, "Whoever heard of such a thing! Students who ought to be spending their time getting an education are out on the street protesting against the government!" I remember at the time saying, "Such a thing would not happen in the United States because young people are too busy getting an education."

As you know, 1947, '48, '49, were the closing years of the nationalist government and freedom in China, so these student demonstrations were part of the signs of the end of the government in China! In 1949 the communists took over. All freedom to demonstrate ceased. Freedom of speech, freedom of the press, freedom to own property, freedom to direct one's own life, all of these things — writ of habeas corpus, trial by jury, all became part of a bygone life!

It seems it should not be necessary to do a lot of thinking in order to plainly see that the present demonstrations at many of our universities are part of the communist master-plan to disrupt and destroy our society. Oh yes, they try very hard to camouflage it behind such pretense as freedom of speech and freedom of the press, but they all follow the same pattern — they are all tied in to the same program.*

We should recall how Israel, in her jubilant but sinful orgies, was warned by the prophet not to rejoice (Hos. 9:1). Disaster for the nation was imminent, and God's servant was trying to turn the people from silliness to sobriety, from foolishness to faith. He was met with despicable disregard. How utterly impossible it seems to be to de-escalate the increasing momentum of a nation toward inevitable catastrophe. This is America today. Because it hasn't happened, we seem to think it can-

---

* Used by written permission.

not happen.

Someone will complain, "Why look for disaster?" The simple fact is, we do not need to look for disaster. It lurks ominously at the end of the wrong course.

Dispossessed

As we hear the counsel of the Lord against an end-time nation, spiritually called Babylon, a detail is furnished to the portrayal which strikes to the very center of the national economy. "A sword is upon her treasures; and they shall be robbed" (Jer. 50:37). The sword in the text does not speak of an ancient warrior's weapon in felling a foe. It means "to eat down," or more literally "to devour" (*kat-es-thee-o*). What other country has seen so many of the world community ravenously devouring her wealth? A factual illustration may be found in the debts which nations owe us for World War I:

Armenia	$ 40,546.970
Austria	25,141,913
Belgium	488,951,077
Czechoslovakia	189,642,023,
Estonia	28,080,360
France	5,077,723,883
Great Britain	7,324,459,301
Greece	12,217,376
Hungary	3,105,536
Italy	1,112,473,909
Latvia	11,575,976
Lithuania	10,319,255
Poland	348,334,464
Rumania	82,906,849
Russia	659,940,665
Yugoslavia	51,425,218

With interest to June 10, 1973, the overall total due us from these countries is a staggering $18,805,919,420.85 (*World Almanac,* 1974).

The Bible says, "A sword shall be upon her treasures." Since a sword connotes destruction, it undoubtedly is speaking of dispossession of her wealth, and it is termed "robbery." The World War I debts are but one lone item that indicates how the nations of the world are depleting our treasures. What is owed us for World War II, the Korean War, and the Vietnam War, together with enormous amounts of goods sent on credit and not paid for should serve to some extent to reveal the type of subtle robbery which is in progress. If one citizen refused to pay his taxes, rightly due to his country, he would be jailed. Why? Because it is robbery.

An editorial in the *Chicago Tribune* under date of November 2, 1967, states:

> Foreign aid is a major reason why your dollar is losing its purchasing power and the debt-burdened, deficit-ridden United States is in the throes of a money crisis. Foreign aid, including interest on the money we have borrowed to give away, now costs the American people more than ten billion dollars a year.
>
> When this unexampled giveaway madness began in 1954, the dollar was worth 77.3 cents, compared with its purchasing power in January 1940 in spite of wartime inflation, but by August 1967 it had declined to 41.48 cents. Meanwhile the United States had accumulated a net deficit of $33.3 billion in its international balance of payments position by the end of 1966; its gold stock had declined from $24.6 billion at the end of 1949 to $13 billion in August 1967, and its liquid liabilities to foreigners, payable in gold, had increased to $29.5 billion. Now the United States is facing a federal deficit that may exceed $30 billion in this fiscal year, accel-

erated inflation, and a money crisis that could induce foreigners to start a run on our remaining gold stock. [This, of course, developed as predicted.]

Moreover, foreign aid is a major cause of federal deficit financing, which increases inflation and the cost of production and thus adversely affects the competitive trade position of the United States.

In *Cures for the Crises,* James F. O'Neil writes:

Crime, delinquency, drug addiction, poverty, alcoholism, mental illness, and war drained an estimated $310 billion from our economic cost; social problems cause untold fear and suffering for millions of Americans.

In 1967, our expenditures exceeded our receipts by almost exactly ten billion dollars. At the close of 1972 our national debt stood at $450,141,605,312, or $2,177.30 per individual citizen. Any humble, practical-minded person, though not schooled in the intricacies of high finance, would sense that a serious condition exists. Our alarmingly diminishing gold reserves, our deficit spending, our constant giving of what we do not possess, our expensive undeclared wars, our unresponsive debtors, the resulting inflation — all lends itself to the divine description in a very telling manner.

The foregoing sixteen descriptions give an enlightening glimpse of the end-time nation God has in view, and concerning which He requests us to hear about His counsel against it. He promises that judgment will come, and that it will be severe.

Chapter 7

The Curtain Falls

There was a day when Israel was transcendently favored, said to be chosen of the Lord to be "above all the nations that are upon the earth" (Deut. 14:2). She was divinely blessed with prosperity, providential protection, and miraculous interventions. Then, indifference, unconcern, and rebellion began to plague the nation. The heavenly appeals through prophet and priest fell on deaf ears as the covenant people persisted in waywardness. Warnings went unheeded. The inevitable happened. The record tersely states, "Her sun is gone down while it was yet day" (Jer. 15:9). The curtain fell on that highly-favored nation.

Israel, in this respect, could be the prototype of the end-time nation, spiritually called Babylon, which will barter away its privileges by defying a holy God until the inevitable will occur. Judgment will come, but how?

Instrument of Judgment

God usually employs human instrumentality when executing judgment upon nations, Russia being a striking exception when He will magnify and sanctify Himself without human assistance (Ezek. 38:22–23).

Prophecy is that phase of Bible revelation in which God, who knows the end from the beginning, reveals His plans for the future and how those plans will materialize. In the blueprints of eschatology is this specification: "For, lo, I will raise and cause to come up against Babylon an assembly [alliance] of great nations from the north country: and they shall set themselves in array against her" (Jer. 50:9).

The immediate reaction will be this: "Then the heaven and the earth, and all that is therein, shall sing [cry aloud] for Babylon: for the spoilers shall come unto her from the north, saith the LORD" (Jer. 51:48).

All directions in prophecy, not otherwise indicated, are predicated upon the position of Israel. South is south of Israel; north, north of Israel, etc. Russia is always "north" in prophetic locations. Actually, she is geographically north of the United States. And Russia becomes more and more a threat. Capable of putting launching platforms in space for nuclear missiles, she may be doing so even now. She has also announced that she has nuclear potential to penetrate all known defense mechanisms.

> The Soviet Union has developed orbital nuclear missiles with devices enabling them to break through an enemy's missile defenses. . . . An orbital weapon is launched like the various spacecraft. It can be brought down on a pre-selected target. The head portions of these rockets carry devices to break through the enemy's antimissile defenses.
> —*Commercial Appeal,* Memphis, November 18, 1967

The State Department acknowledged the possible truth in this claim. And Russia has vowed she will destroy the United States.

U.S. News and World Report, July 15, 1968, carries this bold headline: "Why Joint Chiefs of Staff Worry Over U.S.

Survival." Then, the first statement made by General Earl G. Wheeler is to this effect: "The most dangerous threat to the United States is posed by the growing Soviet strategic nuclear forces."

Senator Stuart Symington (D Mo.) asked this question of General Wheeler: "Are you not beginning, as Chairman of the Joint Chiefs, to become apprehensive about the survival capacity of the United States if things continue along these present lines?"

General Wheeler replied: "The answer is 'Yes,' Senator. You put your finger on what I believe to be the key point, if these trends continue."

A friend, once walking down a street, came upon two lads who were fighting. The one had wrestled his opponent to the sidewalk and was sitting astride him. Amused because the lad on top was crying for help, our friend asked, "Why are you seeking help? You're on top."

"Yes," replied the lad concernedly, "but I feel him rising."

We are on top financially, militarily, and in many other respects, but there is a growing uneasiness, as reflected in General Wheeler's statement, because Russia is rising. Yet, we must not lose sight of the fact that God Himself is the Agent in invoking terrible and complete judgment on the nation He has described. Whether or not Russia surpasses the U.S. in nuclear ability is really beside the point. If the infinite God moves, no power can withstand Him. If the U.S.A. is indeed in view, she is doomed!

Observe, further, God says "nations" (plural), and terms them "great." Would He be including China with Russia? What other great country would be ideologically compatible? Both are avowed enemies of the U.S.A. Both have nuclear power. While these two countries seem to be at loggerheads today, there is little question that they would join forces in an attempt to eliminate Uncle Sam.

Enemy Characterized

In Jeremiah 50:42, we read: "They are cruel, and will not shew mercy: their voice shall roar like the sea." That is, like Goliath, they will constantly issue threats. Both Russia and China are currently doing this.

And, as for the cruelty of this enemy, it has never been so well known as today. Before the writer are two sizeable booklets printed in the United States Government Printing Offices in Washington by the Committee on UnAmerican Activities (House of Representatives, Eighty-Sixth Congress). They both bear the same title, *The Crimes of Khrushchev.* Not only do these publications purport to prove the inhuman character of such godless leaders, but they clearly reveal the vicious attitude of Russia toward the U.S.A.

Said Nikita S. Khrushchev in Warsaw, April 1955, concerning the United States (and a whole page is given in one of these booklets to this quotation): "We must realize we cannot coexist for a long time. One of us must go to his grave. We do not want to go to the grave. They [meaning Americans] do not want to go to their grave either. So what can be done? We must push them to their grave."

Following are a few excerpts from these booklets:

Mr. Arens: Would you sum up briefly your judgment of Khrushchev and his impending visit?

Mr. Lyon: I'll try. In the first place, the new Soviet boss, despite his homespun exterior, is one of the bloodiest tyrants extant. He has come to power over mountains of corpses. Those of us who roll out the red carpet for him will soon have red faces.

The daughter of Josef Stalin, who defected to our country, has given in writing something of the brutality of her father.

Now take note of this nauseating statement by the leader

of the Communist Party in this very land of ours:

> I dream of the hour when the last Congressman is strangled to death on the guts of the last preacher — and since Christians seem to love to sing about the blood, why not give them a little of it? Slit the throats of their children and drag them over the mourner's bench and the pulpit, and allow them to drown in their own blood; and then see whether they enjoy singing these hymns.
>
> —*Sword of the Lord*, April 20, 1962

Says *U.S. News and World Report* (July 15, 1968):

> Never in modern history have prisoners of war been treated the way Americans are treated by the Vietnamese communists. Reds in Vietnam defy the accepted rules of warfare. Prisoners are isolated, often abused, rarely identified by the enemy. Torture has been used to try to make prisoners talk. In one form, a man's ankles are bound and his legs pulled up behind him. The other end of the rope is looped around his neck. A man who struggles or tries to straighten his cramped legs runs the risk of strangling himself.

The returning prisoners of war related heart-rending accounts of their torture.

Did God exaggerate when He said the enemy is cruel! Does God ever exaggerate? *Never!*

Nature of Attack

1. *It will be sudden — a sneak attack.* "O babylon, and thou wast not aware: thou art found, and also caught" (Jer. 50:24). Analyze these words. "Not aware" means complacent, self-assured. "Caught" spells *finis*. This is her demise, and God has already written her obituary.

2. *Paralyzing sabotage.* "The passages are stopped . . . and the men of war [military leaders] are affrighted" (Jer. 51:32). "Passages" probably suggests means of communication, and the word "stopped" means "to cut off." Radio, television, telephone, and telegraph can be cut off suddenly — all perhaps accomplished by a national blackout of electricity. This is a painful possibility. We had an alarming taste of such an experience a year or more ago in the New York City area, with confusion, inconvenience, and frustration indescribable. Multiply this by continent-wide proportions. What would be the reaction?

The statement says, "men of war are affrighted." This word has strong suggestions, such as, tremble inwardly, be alarmed, to hasten, to be anxious, to be amazed, to be dismayed, to be troubled, to be vexed. If such a situation were to develop in our fair land, not only would national and civic leaders be frustrated, but military personnel would be discomfited. And something of this nature verily will happen to some great nation.

3. *The enemy's effective strategy.* "Their arrows shall be as of a mighty expert man; none shall return in vain" (Jer. 50:9). The missiles, like perfectly aimed arrows, will not miss their targets.

4. *Total devastation will ensue.* Note this solemn divine declaration: "Babylon is suddenly fallen and destroyed" (Jer. 51:8). Not just defeated; not just hurt; but destroyed! Sounds utterly inconceivable for any nation, and unthinkable for the U.S.A. But it may be the confronting probability.

5. *An irreparable loss.* To make this a bit more understandable, the Bible directs our attention to a former day when judgment fell: "As God overthrew Sodom and Gomorrah and the neighbuor cities thereof, saith the LORD" (Jer. 50:40). If we can read this aright, the nation in view will

be left a shambles, totally uninhabitable, together with adjacent cities (countries), not only because of wanton, unimaginable destruction, but also apparently because of radioactive fallout and oxygen loss.

6. *Worldwide reaction.* This indescribable catastrophe will be lamented far and wide: "And the cry is heard among the nations" (Jer. 50:46). Again, in Revelation 18:11, "And the merchants of the earth shall weep and mourn over her." The reader would experience much difficulty in trying to convince himself that this has to do with ancient Babylon.

7. *Rapidity of this devastation.* This catastrophic judgment will be over in one hour. "Alas, alas, that great city Babylon, that mighty city [nation in the parent verse in Jeremiah]! for in one hour is thy judgment come. . . . For in one hour so great riches is come to nought. . . . For in one hour is she made desolate" (Rev. 18:10, 17, 19). We have no choice but to construe this thrice-repeated "hour" as literal. The swiftness of the Israeli-Arab war (June 1967) will seem in comparison like an eon. This is the destructive potential of present-day nuclear weapons.

The Nation's Business (May 1968) revealed:

> Russia apparently is flight-testing in secret a means for putting warheads into orbit to float menacingly through space until the Soviet Union is ready to drop them. The capability to station bombs indefinitely in space creates a new sophisticated weapon we'd have to contend with. Russia already has developed what's called a fractional orbital bombardment system which puts a warhead into a low orbit to be ordered down before it completes a full circuit.

In citing these chilling statistics, we are not intimating that our leaders, charged with the defense of our country, are asleep at the switch, or that they are in any way remiss in attempting to meet these mounting threats. They have done and are doing a great deal more than can be made public. Nor are we willfully pessimistic, but when the infinite God, who stakes His holiness on the integrity of His Word, says a nation will go down under His mighty hand of judgment, there is no defense. And so it will be for a certain end-time nation, spiritually called Babylon — a country that gambles on its own strength and forsakes God.

If the wealthy, powerful, wicked, God-forsaking end-time nation, spiritually called Babylon in prophecy, and which is to be visited by this devastating judgment, is indeed the U.S.A., then perhaps this is the answer of the oft-raised question, How can Russia, the king of the north (Dan. 11:40), invade Israel without American protest or intervention? Of course, in such an event, though hideous the thought, she would no longer exist.

Following is an excerpt from a speech in the House of Representatives, as reported by *U.S. News and World Report*, July 31, 1967. In it, the legislator envisioned the possibility of a nuclear attack against our country.

At precisely two in the afternoon of a clear fall day, almost the entire states of Massachusetts, Rhode Island, and New Jersey burst into flames; so did New York City, Hartford, Philadelphia, Baltimore, Washington, D.C. . . . the entire east coast from Portland, Maine, to Norfolk, Virginia, up to one hundred fifty miles inland became a raging, all-consuming fire storm.

At the same moment, a one hundred seventy-mile-wide, twenty-five hundred mile circle of flame erupted in the southern portions of Louisiana, Mississippi, and Alabama . . . destroying all within it. Detroit, Toledo, and half of Ohio met a similar single fate, as did portions of Wisconsin, Illinois, and Indiana, from Milwaukee through Chicago, on to Gary and South Bend.

On the Pacific Coast, flames consumed Portland and Seattle, and everything between them. A fiery torch descended on California's northern population and industrial centers of San Francisco, Oakland, etc.

Simultaneously, nine million Southern Californians, including another major fraction of the nation's scientific and industrial talent, were incinerated in a band of fire from Oxnard, north of Los Angeles, to San Diego and the Mexican border.

Three one-hundred-megaton bombs, optimized for thermal-heat-radiation, had exploded at altitudes below fifty thousand feet to create the East Coast conflagration, and over each of the other six areas described, one more had detonated. At the same instant, eight one-hundred-megaton monsters had burst and spread over U.S. ICBM [intercontinental ballistic missile] complexes in the triangle from Arkansas to Montana to Arizona, incidentally igniting Phoenix, Tucson, Little Rock, Wichita, Cheyenne, Kansas City, Great Falls and many more cities.

The 18th hostile warhead exploded 4,000 feet below the waters of the Pacific on slopes of the Aleutian Deep. It created a tidal wave 28 to 70 feet high. . . . Fire storms — a hundred times more intense than World War Two's which consumed Hamburg and other German cities — raged in part or all of 34 of the 50 states.

Considerable loss of life outside the fire storms occurred from suffocation. Major casualties also resulted from winds of more than hurricane proportions, feeding oxygen to the blazes. In all, a fair portion of the continent's oxygen was used up by combustion. Not enough was left in many places to support life. . . . Three of every five Americans were dead and the nation's military-industrial back was broken.

In this most graphic and dramatic imaginative description, the congressman said if Russia hit the United States with one hundred megaton bombs, it would utterly destroy this nation. Who can assure that this will not happen? We were struck at Pearl Harbor.

Time of Development

Timetables in prophecy are not always readily deciphered. We are sometimes forced to view patterns of prophesied developments, and then to correlate the factors within the given pattern. This we know, however, the divine plan, among other important matters, calls for the elimination of religious Babylon, political Babylon*, and Russia, and, we believe, in this precise order. Thus, if God is going to use Russia to destroy political Babylon, then obviously political Babylon must go down before Russia is eliminated. Then, when will Russia be eliminated?

Jehovah determines seventy weeks of years, or four hundred ninety years, in His dealings with Israel. Sixty-nine of those weeks were fulfilled when Christ was rejected and crucified. One week of seven years remains to be completed. It is variously termed the Tribulation, the day of Jacob's trouble, the day of the wrath of God. It is divided into two equal parts of three and one-half years, or forty-two months.

Since Russia will be supernaturally disposed of at the time of her invasion of Israel and Egypt (Ezek. 38:22; Dan. 11:40–45), and in the same manner as were Sodom and Gomorrah, and if we are justified in believing that the coming world dictator is at that time mortally wounded and resurrected as was Jesus, concerning whom he is the anti-type, and since power

---

* That political Babylon is contemporary with the ultimate development of the false church and modern Russia is a powerful proof that the Babylon prophesied in Jeremiah 50–51 and Revelation 18 is this projected entity.

is given to him to continue for forty-two months (Rev. 13:5), then the judgment of the nation spiritually called Babylon must precede the downfall of Russia if Russia is to be the divine instrument of that judgment. The end of religious Babylon will have taken place even earlier. The time, then, for political Babylon's desolation will be sometime in the first half of Daniel's seventieth week.

This leads us to a very logical and most reassuring conclusion — the true church will not be here at that time. Comprised of genuine believers in the Lord, wherever they may be found, the church will have been evacuated — raptured from the earth to heaven (1 Thess. 4:16–17). That is not to say she will not see hard times. Pressure is constantly being brought to bear upon the people of God, but the church will certainly be spared from this inevitable national disaster. This is not simply preferential attention; it is by virtue of what seems to be the prophetic program, for the judgment of political Babylon is in Revelation 18 and the church is not found from Revelation 4 to 19.

Further, if the U.S.A. is eliminated by Russia, Russia's ultimate defeat must of necessity be supernatural (Ezek. 38:22–23), for there would be no earthly power capable of subduing her. Assuming that the U.S.A. is removed from the scene, Russia's only obstacle in her avowed quest for world domination would be the ten-kingdom power out of Europe, oftentimes referred to as the revival of the old Roman Empire, and about which the Scriptures are so impressively explicit.

Hence, the "king of the north" (Russia) will put at him, the head of the final and powerful ten-kingdom confederation out of Europe as found in Daniel 11:40. At that time, the King of Glory will step into the picture, will put hooks into his jaws (Ezek. 38:4), and will destroy him utterly (Dan. 11:45; Ezek. 38:22–23). Five-sixths of his forces will be killed, and the Israelites will be seven months burying the dead (Ezek. 39:12).

The world's worst and last dictator, indwelt by the Devil himself and receiving his power, throne, and authority (Rev. 13:2), will prosper in his unprecedented nefarious acts until he is destroyed by the Lord in His second advent (2 Thess. 2:8).

Chapter 8

No Suspension of Reason

Has anyone's intellect ever been thwarted who believed the Bible? Never! Has anyone ever gone astray morally who practiced biblical precepts? Unthinkable! One does not forsake reason who embraces truth. It is interesting to hear Jehovah saying to decadent Israel, "Come now, and let us reason together" (Isa. 1:18). Such reasoning fortifies the inner being, strengthens conviction, and inspires the noblest ideals. Unbelief, on the other hand, prevents vision, perverts privilege, and precludes providential blessing.

Internal Deterioration

A lyrical expression in the favorite old hymn, "Abide With Me," states: "Change and decay in all around I see." But how does one explain the inherent principle of destruction? A body becomes saturated with malignancy, a carcass seethes with maggots, a fruit turns brown with rot, a nation crumbles with insidious corruption.

The Bible tells us that "we wrestle not against flesh and blood, but against principalities, against powers, against the rulers of the darkness of this world, against spiritual wickedness in high places" (Eph. 6:12). This is something of a *Celes-*

tial Intelligence report, informing us of the enemy's tactical procedure. His combative forces fall into four classifications — principalities, powers, rulers of darkness, and wicked spirits in high places.

Principalities connotes Satan's top brass, the pentagon of perversity, the citadel of infamy — a demoniacal scheme to destroy authority from the empire down to the home. One need not wonder what unseen forces are at work in a national scandal like Watergate, or in a schismatic disruption in a prestigious church, or in the utter loss of parental control in a well-established home. Here is the answer. And the breakdown of authority is the precursor of anarchy. Thus the author of confusion presses his battle.

The U.S. government, loudly acclaimed as the most powerful on earth, prosecuted seven serious criminal cases in recent years, and lost them all in spite of evident guilt. It is unbelievable that men can destroy government property right in the nation's capital, steal highly sensitive records, turn courtrooms into circuses, then go stark free.

Powers points up the enemy's arsenal of energy, a diabolical task force of demons to slay chastity, integrity, credibility, and honor, with derelicts of humanity strewn over the battlefield of life as proof of his devastating successes. In every age, some of the most trusted people are plunged into the dismal darkness of disgrace by these overpowering forces, to languish in shame and defeat.

Rulers of the darkness foment and foster everything sinister, weird, and eerie. These demons are the extinguishers of light in the experience of unsuspecting people, or even in those who are aware of the caprice of the tempter, but who, failing to flee his temptation, fall victim to the overwhelming force with which they cannot cope. When the president's counsel was asked for an explanation of the gap in a tape recording, he replied, "It must have been some sinister force." His statement was perhaps more correct than convincing. Evil spirits, through human instrumentality, do their utmost to injure, mislead, confuse, and depress.

What makes internal deterioration so insidious and so dangerous is that, like malignancy, its presence may not be manifested before it exacts its toll. An enemy is easier detected on the battlefield than a saboteur in a manufacturing plant. Disloyalty in a high office or in the citadel of learning, like disease germs in the anatomy, can weaken the structure of a nation's well-being. And it does not need to operate rapidly to be effective. Subtlety moves slowly and stealthily. "A little leaven leaveneth the whole lump." The bacterial count in moral corruption can be as alarming in the body politic as in the body corporeal, and our country is being shaken profoundly by the discovery of widespread moral turpitude in leadership. It is a bad omen.

It is a bad omen because it threatens a cessation of divine blessings. When the hand of Providence is withdrawn, what can finite, limited, dependent creatures do? Where do we turn? Self-sufficiency for which we strive is an impossibility. Man is but a prospector. He can't create. He can only work with that which is given to him. He sees a rabbit. He didn't put it there, but he shoots it. He sees a tree. He didn't put it there, but he cuts it down. He sees sod. He didn't put it there, but he plows it up. He reaps where he has not sowed.

If we want to shore up our defenses, it is absolutely imperative, an impelling necessity, that we give more attention to the spiritual standards which are so indelibly inscribed on the statutes of Holy Writ, for when there is a spiritual breakdown such as we as a nation are now witnessing, there will be a moral breakdown. This is the case against political Babylon.

Not an Empty Theory

It would seem most improbable for one, no matter his hermeneutical knowledge or exegetical ability, to compress all the Babylon matter of Jeremiah 50 and 51 into the mold of history and label it "Fulfilled."

Thus, this image of an end-time nation, spiritually called Babylon, is more than a mirage on the surface of an author's imagination. It is there irrefutably and irremovably on the pages of Sacred Writ. The Holy Spirit has painted the picture. Its colors are true. Its brush strokes are accurate. The fundamental image is established for all who have eyes to see. The perspective is clear.

However, since similarities at times may be coincidental rather than substantiating, we may be reluctant to title the portrait in terms of a modern nation. But no one can lightly dismiss the possibility of its being the nation which we love. We do not avow that it is. On the other hand, with the facts thoroughly pondered, one would hesitate to declare flatly that it is not.

On what comfortable and convenient grounds may the U.S.A. claim immunity from divine judgment? "The nation that forgets God goes backward" — backward to defeat, backward to destruction. That we as a nation are going backward cannot be denied. We are regressing spiritually, morally, legally, financially, governmentally, and that with alarming acceleration. It is only natural, of course, to abhor any suggestion of national disaster. This was the bitter reaction of the people in Jeremiah's day. He prophesied with great compassion that judgment would befall the nation, that the "city of peace" would be razed. He was cast into a miry dungeon by angry mobs who were vociferous in denying that such a thing could be true and in claiming that the preacher was suffering from a neurosis. But it *did* come to pass!

The Lord told Daniel in stranger language than He employs in Jeremiah 50 and 51 and in Revelation 18 that judgment would come to his nation. The picture was painted in complicated imagery. There was a little horn, a ram, a goat, etc. There was also a king of fierce countenance, the terrible Antiochus Epiphanes. In spite of the striking visions and stirring imagery, Daniel knew that God was telling him something actual, something severe; that catastrophic judgments would come. He believed God. He knew that horrendous developments were in the offing, and this was his reaction: "I Daniel fainted, and was sick certain days. . . . I Daniel was grieved in my spirit . . . my countenance changed in me."

One is not a prophet of gloom, a pestilential pessimist, a draper of dismay, or a crepehanger who believes God's judicial pronouncements and dares to make then known. General aversion to such facts furnishes no escape, nor is violent objection in any wise a detente. God's justice cannot be deterred. "He is faithful who hath promised and he will do it."

Said the renowned Gen. William K. Harrison:

> I do not know a nation of modern times that deserves the judgment of a holy God as much as America. No other nation has been granted such physical blessings, such spiritual, and such political freedom, yet it has become pagan in character.

Divine judgment of some form seems inevitable.

It is quite noteworthy that, rather suddenly, there are frequent allusions to the United States as "modern Babylon." The following excerpts are examples in point:

Under the caption, "Eldridge Cleaver's War with Babylon," and datelined Algiers, we read:

> Eldridge Cleaver declared here Tuesday that he intends to expand his group of overseas Black Panthers into an international operation dedicated to overthrowing the U.S. government. Cleaver declared, "Our job is to destroy Babylon."

How did he define Babylon? "'Just like it says in the Bible,' he answered. 'It is a symbol of decadence and corruption. . . .'" (*Chicago Sun-Times,* October 26, 1970).

Also, dateline Block Island, Rhode Island:

> Witnessing what he describes as the decline and fall of the United States, William Stringfellow shouts "Hallelujah!" [Stringfellow is a Harvard Law School graduate and a former practicing attorney.] To Stringfellow, the United States is the modern equivalent of Babylon, the "most rich and powerful of all nations which underwent a process of violent disintegration."
>
> —*Chicago Sun-Times,* October 31, 1970

Thus, contemporaries believe the Bible to designate the U.S.A. as "Babylon," and are increasingly vocal in so terming it.

A Prominent Name

The word "Babylon" is legendary. When it appears in print or falls from a speaker's lips, myriads of concepts flash across the screen of one's thoughts. There is the Tower of Belus with the fantastic dreams of its erectors — a tower pushing heavenward. Or,

There is the ancient empire with Nebuchadnezzar enthroned in his glorious dominion as the head of gold, the initial monarch, holding a scepter over the whole world in Gentile sovereignty. Or,

The great city which etched itself into the fabric of history with an almost singular design, the center of commerce — the envy of mankind. Or yet,

A woman arrayed in purple and scarlet, decked with gold and silver and pearls and scintillating gems, holding a golden chalice — the fantasy of ecumenicists, a dream come true for religionists. Or even yet,

An ethnic entity with blazing colors of grandeur, fabulous in her wealth, unrivaled in her scientific achievements, obsessed with her lusts, transcendent in her power.

But all that has the *hallmark* of Babylon must be purged from the earth. And God will do it! As for historical Babylon, He said, "Go to, let us go down, and there confound their language. . . . So the LORD scattered them abroad" (Gen. 11:7–8).

As for religious Babylon (the final form of religious organization), the ten-horned kingdom of Antichrist will outlaw it, and destroy it, and expropriate its vast resources (Rev. 17:16), for God hath put it in their hearts to fulfill His will (Rev. 17:17).

And, as for political Babylon, a powerful, prosperous, prestigious end-time nation, she will go down to destruction even as religious Babylon will have gone (Rev. 17:18), and the agent in this regard, as in all other instances, is none other than God Himself. "From me shall spoilers come unto her, saith the LORD" (Jer. 51:53).

That the stamp of Babylon and the subtlety of Babylon and the stigma of Babylon must be completely eradicated should be most evident to those who know the Scriptures. As was pointed out earlier in this volume, the basic concept in the Babylon doctrine is twofold. First, to contradict all that God says; and, second, to counteract all that God does. Nor does it matter whether this satanic subtlety is inherent in a religious body or in a nation. It is anti-Christ, and "he [Christ] must reign, till he hath put *all* enemies under his feet" (1 Cor. 15:25).

As the word "Baal" became colloquial in Old Testament times referring to all types of idolatry (usually in the plural, Baalim), even so the word "Babylon" throughout the ages has been employed to connote intemperance, lustfulness, and unspirituality. Journalists speak of America as "living a Babylon existence."

The total triumph of our blessed Lord guarantees the elimination of everything which militates against His holiness. He will purge the Holy of Holies of the foul presence of the image of the Antichrist. He will cast the Devil into the lake of fire. He will purge out the rebels of Israel (Ezek. 20:38). He will judge the Gentile nations, turning the unbelieving into everlasting destruction. He will remove the curse from the earth.

All of this purging and purifying in His redemptive scheme would not and could not be complete if the whole Babylon issue were not settled fully and forever. This will not be accomplished in one stroke of judgment. The divine plan, clearly set forth, calls for, among other things, the termination of religious Babylon, the final form of church organization with all its confusing and empty doctrines, and the destruction of political Babylon which is a prosperous end-time nation that gradually but surely ruled the Lord of glory out of its national structure.

Lack of Embellishments

The picture is not completed. There are more descriptions, but the fundamental image seems to be evident, at least developed to the point of usefulness for the purpose at hand. It may be studied for perspective and expression. It is a word portrait silhouetted on the horizon of eschatology, and has to do with a terrifying probability for a particular nation. It is a picture the colors of which blend into a commanding image, and cannot but arrest the careful attention of thinking people.

Should there arise in the reader's mind a question about the abbreviated quotations of Bible references in the foregoing descriptions, may we offer this brief explanation: It was so done, not unwittingly, but with purpose, (1) to conserve space in this limited volume, and (2) to emphasize the descriptive characteristics which might not have been as apparent and as illuminating in the midst of greater verbosity.

In justification of this procedure, we would call attention to the fact that, in many instances in the sacred Scriptures, an entire verse may not prove to be a completed statement. In Ephesians 1, for instance, it is necessary to cover twelve verses (three through fourteen) to complete one full sentence. Yet it must be granted that it is not uncommon for messages to be built on one of these verses or a fraction thereof. This is not being "partial in the law" (Mal. 2:9), especially when the purpose is properly and accurately served.

Most particularly, however, one verse may present two or more unrelated facts, or facts that are widely separated in application. An illustration in point is found in Isaiah 61:2 where a comma divides the verse by more than nineteen hundred years. It is this: "To proclaim the acceptable year of the Lord, and the day of vengeance of our God." The first part of this verse is history; the second, prophecy. In quoting, Jesus used only the first part as He was initiating His earthly ministry (Luke 4:19).

The imaged entity, spiritually called Babylon, does not require embellishment; just sufficient fact for a possible identification. Then, we are able to look in the right direction, to say the least, and to ponder with greater understanding the subject divinely portrayed. We find ourselves then in a position to hear the counsel God has taken against the nation described, which counsel He requests all people to hear and believe. This is the main purpose of this volume.

All the Gentiles nations will ultimately face the judgment of God for a termination of their national existence (Dan. 2:34–35); but, we repeat, two powerful countries are definitely singled out for an earlier demise than the others. Russia most certainly is one; the other is a nation spiritually called Babylon. It is a nation that must inevitably and accurately fit the foregoing description.

Further enlightening details are available. Their inclusion naturally would lend convincing force to our presentation, but space limitations preclude this. It is our wish the material furnished will add up to a case that will command attention and retain interest. The solemnity of the overall implications is intended not to depress or frighten, but to alert and arouse.

We urgently need to be apprised of the apparent probability which confronts our beloved nation in its ill-advised course, and we must be speedily awakened out of our dreadful indifference toward the holy standards of righteousness which alone can promise a future.

It is not that the author desires to be a self-styled Paul Revere. He is simply a conscientious sharer of discovered suggestions in the divine Record and a willing transmitter of the same for a timely challenge to those of an open mind. Thus, this matter is presented, not with the thought of provoking argument, but with the hope of producing concern.

A Recapitulation

The period of Gentile dominion had a specific beginning (Dan. 2:37). This period will have a definite termination (Dan. 2:34). It is firmly established and plainly revealed that the Lord of glory will wind up the affairs of the nations, and will Himself institute His own government and reign in righteousness over the whole earth (Isa. 2:4). It is noteworthy in this connection, however, that the Spirit of Truth lists certain nations to fall by divine judgment prior to the total collapse of Gentile dominion which will take place when the Lord returns to this earth.

Particularly cited are two great sovereign states which will have especially incurred the indignation of the Lord. The one is "the king of the north" or Russia (Ezek. 38:22). But prior to this nation's demise, another of even greater prominence is slated for the consuming vengeance of the Lord. This nation is spiritually called "Babylon."

Historical Babylon is to eventuate in two imposing branches, viz., religious Babylon, the ultimate of organized religion, and prophetical, political Babylon, a powerful but God–forsaking end-time nation.

God will put it into the hearts of Antichrist's ten kingdoms to utterly eliminate the "woman" or the false church, which is religious Babylon (Rev. 17:16–17). He also will take counsel against prophetical, political Babylon and will cause a great nation from the "north" to destroy her.

Before this judgment falls, God will call for His people (those saved in the early part of Daniel's seventieth week) to flee this doomed nation and emigrate to Zion or Israel (Jer. 50:28).

Since unnamed entities in prophecy, such as the Antichrist, may be identified by description, and since this end-time nation is not specifically named, we are obliged to search for its description which, obviously, is quite prolific. Some of the given characteristics are as follows:

1. She is the offspring of a kingdom which will deteriorate from a position of world leadership.
2. She at one time was a cup of gold in the Lord's hand — a monetary instrument in the promotion of God's work.
3. She has a cosmopolitan population — a "mingled people."
4. She is the latest or youngest of nations, said to be "the hindermost."
5. She is an exceedingly wealthy country — "abundant in treasures."
6. She is the most powerful nation and termed "the hammer of the whole earth."
7. Her scientific achievements excel all other nations.
8. She speaks with an influential voice in the world community.

9. She has established unprecedented national defenses.
10. She involves herself in global affairs.
11. She is singularly and lavishly generous in foreign aid.
12. She has the highest standard of living, even of an epicurean character.
13. She becomes a spiritual renegade, lapsing into idolatry and covetousness.
14. Through unrestrained permissiveness, a moral decadence ensues to the proportions of blatant turpitude.
15. She develops pride and haughtiness through egotistical bias and claims to "sit a queen," untouched by defeat and untouchable.
16. The "unsinkable titanic" of nations is slowly, subtly, and surely stripped of her gold.

Some end-time nation will answer to these descriptions. That nation, having been mightily blessed of God, will incur His indignation because of her godlessness. And when the hour of divine judgment arrives, an alliance of greater nations from the prophetical "north," possessing devastating, vulnerable weapons in formidable quantities, will strike unexpectedly, suddenly, and decisively.

As the "woman" (the false church) shall be utterly eliminated, even so, the end-time nation, spiritually called Babylon, shall irreparably perish from the earth. Her beauty and pride shall no more restrain the hand of divine judgment than the impressiveness of Lucifer, the son of the morning, could prevent his fall and ultimate doom when he turned from God and through pride exalted himself.

Chapter 9
A Glimpse of Modern America

The portents on the horizon are most disturbing. The fierce clashes of conflicting ideologies, ruthless subversive tactics, the violent quest for power, the uprisings of minorities — all combine with myriads of other disconcerting factors to becloud the atmosphere.

Add to this the current racial demonstrations, the restlessness of the underprivileged, together with the constant increase of immorality and crime, of corruption in high places, of multiplying espionage agents (which can be counted but not captured), the prevailing lawlessness, the looting of property and burning of buildings, the fuel crisis, the disintegration of home life, the prevalence of juvenile delinquency, the fickleness of fads, and the rapidly declining influence of the church. The picture is a somber one!'

And the outlook is not bright. An article in the *St. Petersburg Times* stated in part:

In order to assure itself of large audiences, television must rely on adult pictures with their increasing emphasis on sex, nudity, and violence. In short, when the issue comes down to a choice between profit and morality, profit in the long run almost always wins. It is just a question of time before anything goes.

The more alarming way to put it is this: It is only a question of time before such a nation, as did Sodom and Gomorrah, goes down under the hand of divine judgment, and for the same reason.

Lord Byron said: "Civilization goes like this: First freedom, and then glory, and then wealth, and then vice, and then corruption, and then barbarism, and then collapse."

Whatever he may have had in mind, the late President Kennedy said in his State of the Union message: "Each day we draw nearer to the hour of maximum danger."

Dr. Robert Munger put it this way: "We stand at the crossroads of destiny confronted by a chaotic world on the brink of self-destruction."

Dr. Robert Shuller adds: "The survival of America is at stake."

There is a growing universal obsession that finite man with advanced technological knowledge, supersonic transportation, and instantaneous global communication can bring about a *Utopia* on this earth. It is a grandiose scheme — appealing, challenging, convincing. It calls for *one* world, *one* government, *one* church, but this enlarging bubble is doomed to burst.

The Bible states that "when they shall say, Peace and safety; then sudden destruction cometh upon them, as travail upon a woman with child." Man has neither the foundation on which to build such a glorious situation, nor the right kind of material. "A society predicated on a false premise is predoomed" (Paul Harvey). And history is replete with examples — civilizations buried under their own ruins.

Make no mistake, the great and pressing need of the hour for us as individuals and as a nation is to get back to spiritual basics — back where the soul of man can find confidence as foundations crumble about us. And the way back is the way of the Bible. It is, and ever shall be, "a lamp unto my feet, and a light unto my* path." Its hallowed illumination leads into the way "of the just which shines more and more unto the perfect day."

It may be the eleventh hour, but many a fight has been won in the last round. If the reader does not know the plan for his personal salvation and his spiritual responsibility to others, ascertain it speedily! Then, with vigor, courage, and honesty, as our noble forebears, fight the good fight of faith. Victory is not only preferable to defeat, it is absolutely possible under God!

In one of Israel's darkest days of old, Jehovah said, "If my people, which are called by my name, shall humble themselves, and pray, and seek my face, and turn from their wicked ways; then will I hear from heaven, and will forgive their sin, and will heal their land" (2 Chron. 7:14).

If our nation would accept this challenge, there would be no question about her future. *But* if the present trends continue and increase, she may possibly be the end-time nation to be judged.

It is not our purpose in this presentation to render a verdict or to finalize a conclusion, but simply to adduce evidence. Evidence is the material of proof. Whether or not the proof is irrefutably established in this case, the reader must determine for himself. However, one disturbing question will linger on the horizon of our minds — to what other nation of all time could these divinely-given characteristics and descriptions so convincingly apply?

Those of us whose heartbeat is quickened by the singing of "America the Beautiful" could wish that the end-time nation to be destroyed is not the U.S.A. Those of us whose spirits are moved to see Old Glory waving in the breeze as the martial strains of the National Anthem fill the air are wont to exclaim, "Perish the thought!" But who amongst us is not painfully aware that our great Ship of State is currently in turbulent waters and headed for treacherous shoals? Concern prevails!

View matters as one will, the only security for the individual is absolute faith in the divine plan. It offers freely to all a present assurance and a future hope.

Part Two
Historical Babylon
Versus
Mystery Babylon

by Dr. Noah W. Hutchings

Chapter 10

The City

The unfolding of the chronological course of prophecy to its ultimate conclusion can be compared to a Shakespearean drama where all the main characters in the play emerge once more at the final scene to make a last curtain call. As we look to Europe and the Middle East, we see the European Union as evidence of the revived Roman Empire; the biblical nations of Syria, Egypt, Ethiopia, Greece, Iran (or Persia), Arabia, and Gog (or Russia), are in their proper prophetic places. Israel is back in the Land of Promise. We also see Jordan, comprising the ancient nations of Ammon, Moab, and Edom, ready to fulfill its destiny during the Great Tribulation as prophesied by Daniel. But what about one of the most powerful empires that was prominent in biblical times, the nation that was the very genesis of the "times of the Gentiles," Babylon?

It is certain that Babylon is to play a major role in world events during the last days. From chapters fifty through fifty-two of Jeremiah, and chapters seventeen through nineteen in the Book of Revelation, Babylon is mentioned during the Great Tribulation as being a city, a nation, a commercial power, and a religious system. There is no mystery about Israel being established again as a nation in 1948; there is no mystery about

Syria, Egypt, and the other nations in their end-time setting. So why is the identity of Babylon in the last days called a mystery? It would seem that it is called a mystery because its various identities are hidden from the general understanding of the world.

Perhaps the least mysterious aspect of the multifaceted Babylon of the last days is the city itself. But even so, as we see the attempt being made to restore this ancient metropolis to its former glory, most biblical and historical scholars doubt and wonder that this can ever be accomplished. In 1971 plans were announced by Iraq to rebuild Babylon according to its ancient architectural designs. Funds for the project were to be provided by Iraq, UNESCO, and the Arab oil barons of the Middle East. When we were in Babylon in 1978, the ruins were being excavated, and the theater of Nebuchadnezzar had been restored, as well as several of the temples and other buildings.

Two years after we were in Babylon, the war between Iraq and Iran erupted and continued for eight years. Although the war slowed the rebuilding of Babylon, it was not entirely stopped. The January 16, 1987, edition of the *Los Angeles Times* included an article entitled "New Writing on Wall — CAN BABYLON RELIVE ITS GLORY DAYS?" I quote:

> "In the same hour came forth fingers of a man's hand, and wrote . . . upon the plaster of the wall of the king's palace. . . . And this is the writing that was written. . . . God hath numbered thy kingdom, and finished it. . . . Thou art weighed in the balances, and art found wanting" (Dan. 5).
>
> There is still handwriting on the wall of Nebuchadnezzar's palace. Not as apocalyptic as the message that the Bible says Daniel translated to King Belshazzar, it simply proclaims to all who pass through the portals of these time-worn ruins that "Pete was here." Today, little remains of the grandeur that was ancient Babylon, the city of Hammu-

rabi and Nebuchadnezzar, the site of the Hanging Gardens and the Tower of Babel, and, of course, the place where the famous handwriting on the wall spoiled Belshazzar's dinner party. Nowadays graffiti deface what is left of the walls. . . . In a way, it is perversely fitting. In the reconstructed Temple of Emach, graffiti in a veritable Babel of languages clutter the restored whitewashed walls. . . .

The present intrudes upon Babylon in other ways too. At the entrance to the ruins, next to a half-size model of the great Ishtar Gate, stands a thirty-foot-high portrait of Iraqi president Saddam Hussein, shown there as a modern-day Nebuchadnezzar protecting Babylon from its past and present enemies, the Persians of neighboring Iran. At a time when Iraq is hard-pressed to continue paying for the cost of its six-year-old war with Iran, Hussein has ordered that no expense be spared to restore ancient Babylon to its former glory in time for an international music festival that is scheduled to be held here in September. The restoration project, begun in 1978 before the start of the Iran-Iraq War, was undertaken to save the remnants of the city. . . .

However, Babylon has assumed additional importance for the government since the war broke out in September 1980. Keen on establishing a link between its current conflict with the Persians and the legendary battles of the past, the Iraqi government speeded up the reconstruction in order to make Babylon a symbol of national pride. In the haste, however, some Western critics suggest that Babylon is not so much being restored to its former glory as it is being turned into a three-dimensional propaganda statement. . . .

Iraqi officials bridle at criticisms like this and say when the reconstruction is finished, the new Babylon will look just like the old one. . . .

"Many, many things have been stolen from Babylon," said Munir Bashir, an internationally known musician who is supervising the organization of the Babylon Music Festival. "We have asked for these things back, but it is impossible," he added regretfully. Bashir, who plays the lute and the ud, has ambitious plans for the music festival to be held in the restored amphitheater and other made-over parts of the two thousand-year-old ruins from September 22 to October 22. "We will have musicians from all over the world, from Europe, Asia, Africa, and Arabia. From America we will have a famous movie star — I cannot say which one yet — and we have asked Madonna," he said.

Why Madonna? "Because the Iraqi young people love Madonna. Madonna lives here with the Iraqi people," he added, pointing to his heart. "I hope Madonna will know this fact and will come."

U.S. officials, hoping that a still-active cultural exchange program with Iraq can keep alive relations that fell into something of a political coma after the disclosures of U.S. arms sales to Iran, are trying to recruit American talent for the festival. However, Western diplomats express concern that the Iraqis may be in for a disappointment when it comes to getting big-name U.S. talent. "The Iraqis want this to be a great festival, like Baalbek in the old days," one diplomat said. "But with the war on, a lot of people are going to be afraid to come."

Bashir dismisses these fears as unfounded, noting that Babylon, fifty-five miles south of Baghdad on the Euphrates River, is well away from any fighting and has never been bombed. "Babylon is completely safe," he said. Also, "this is not just an Iraqi festival," he added, warming to his favorite subject. "It is a festival for the whole world, because Babylon was the capital of civilization once and has given the world so much. People from all over want to come to Babylon."

Talent already signed up for the festival includes ballet

troupes from the Soviet Union and France, opera from Italy, folk dancers from Greece, Turkey, Poland, and Yugoslavia, flamenco artists from Spain, and Bedouin dancers from Saudi Arabia.

"The movie stars who are our guests will each recite the laws of Hammurabi in their own languages," Bashir said. "Everything will be like it was in ancient Babylon," he added. "People will be given Babylonian costumes to wear and newly minted Babylonian money to spend." Even the food to be served will be based on two thousand-year-old recipes, he said.

The Babylon . . . construction workers are rebuilding . . . the Babylon of Nebuchadnezzar, who reigned from 605 to 526 B.C. . . .

The city rising somewhat hurriedly from the ruins in time for the festival is also the one that got such bad reviews in the Bible as the "mother of harlots and of earth's abominations," a reputation that Bashir says is unfair. . . . And although he does not think of it in quite these terms, what Bashir really wants to do is to prove that the Bible was wrong. For in bringing together musicians from around the world to perform here, Bashir is attempting to grant Babylon a pardon from the biblical sentence imposed upon it in the Book of Revelation, when a "mighty angel cast a stone into the sea and said: So shall Babylon the great city be thrown down with violence, and shall be found no more: and the sound of harpers and minstrels, of flute players and trumpeters, shall be heard in thee no more."

Why would Saddam Hussein designate millions of dollars to the rebuilding of an old city that has apparently no commercial or social value, especially in the midst of a war? The possible answer to this question may be in a resurgence of Chaldean pride, as Saddam Hussein insisted. But the most definitive reason has to be so that Babylon will be destroyed like Sodom and Gomorrah just before Jesus Christ returns.

The items of importance contained in the *Los Angeles Times* story about the 1987 music festival in Babylon are:

1. A huge portrait of Saddam Hussein stands beside the Ishtar Gate.
2. A command world music festival was chosen to announce the rebirth of Babylon.
3. No expense was to be spared in restoring Babylon to its former glory.
4. The American rock star, Madonna, was specifically requested to be the queen of the festival.
5. They are seeking proof that God is a liar for saying that Babylon would be destroyed in a fiery holocaust.

Babylon was built on the ancient site of Babel, and it was at Babel that the people decided that God was wrong when He commanded them to spread over the face of the earth. They said, "Let us build a tower to heaven and defy God." Nebuchadnezzar defied God, and he was made to eat grass in the fields for seven years until he acknowledged that God was the Most High of both heaven and earth. Belshazzar defied God and defiled the holy vessels taken from the Temple in Jerusalem. Babylon is a historical symbol of man's defiance of the Lord of heaven; therefore, it is no surprise that one reason for this modern Belshazzar-type festival was to defy God's judgment already determined in His Word.

From the Scriptures we know there is music that praises and pleases God. We read in Psalm 150:

Praise ye the LORD. Praise God in his sanctuary: praise him in the firmament of his power. Praise him for his mighty acts: praise him according to his excellent greatness. Praise him with the sound of the trumpet: praise him with the psaltery and harp. Praise him with the timbrel and dance: praise him with stringed instruments and organs. Praise him upon the loud cymbals: praise him upon the high sounding cymbals. Let every thing that hath breath praise the Lord. Praise ye the Lord.

There is also music that is an abomination to God. When Moses came down from Mount Sinai with the Law of God graven on tablets of stone, he heard the sound of such music in the camp of Israel and knew before he arrived at the camp that the people were defying God and worshipping an idol.

The same kind of satanic music was heard in ancient Babylon when Nebuchadnezzar commanded the people who came from all over the empire to fall down and worship his golden image. We read in Daniel 3:14–15:

> Nebuchadnezzar spake and said unto them, Is it true, O Shadrach, Meshach, and Abednego, do not ye serve my gods, nor worship the golden image which I have set up? Now if ye be ready that at what time ye hear the sound of the cornet, flute, harp, sackbut, psaltery, and dulcimer, and all kinds of musick, ye fall down and worship the image which I have made; well: but if ye worship not, ye shall be cast the same hour into the midst of a burning fiery furnace; and who is that God that shall deliver you out of my hands?

It is thought that this idol was erected just to the south of Babylon on a foundational pedestal which is still there. The theater of Nebuchadnezzar was also on the south side of Babylon outside the walls of the city. So it was probably in the king's theater where the musicians played when everyone fell down and worshipped the idol. It seems more than just coincidental that it was in the same theater that the Babylonian music festival was convened on September 22, 1987. With interest we note that Nebuchadnezzar stated that at his music festival there was "all kinds of musick." At the Babylonian music festival in 1987 there was all kinds of music from all over the world, everything from opera to rock music.

In the eighteenth chapter of Revelation, the ultimate and final destruction of the city of Babylon is prophesied — it will be destroyed in one hour with a mighty fiery judgment. We read of the fate of the musicians of Babylon in Revelation 18:20–22:

Rejoice over her, thou heaven, and ye holy apostles and prophets; for God hath avenged you on her. And a mighty angel took up a stone like a great millstone, and cast it into the sea, saying, Thus with violence shall that great city Babylon be thrown down, and shall be found no more at all. And the voice of harpers, and musicians, and of pipers, and trumpeters, shall be heard no more at all in thee; and no craftsman, of whatsoever craft he be, shall be found any more in thee; and the sound of a millstone shall be heard no more at all in thee.

The question of contemporary consideration is whether the Babylon on the Euphrates that has been in a process of restoration for the past thirty years is the Babylon mentioned in Isaiah 13; Jeremiah 50 and 51; and in Revelation 18 and 19 that will be destroyed as were Sodom and Gomorrah in one hour. We will approach this question in more detail, from both the perspective of the 1990 Middle East crisis, and the prophetic Word, in later chapters.

Chapter 11

Babylon B.C.

As we have noted in the previous chapter, the 1987 celebration in Babylon was for the purpose of letting all the world know that Babylon lives again and that God is wrong in His pronouncement of judgment against the city in the last days.

The beginning of the biblical history of Babylon is recorded in Genesis 11:1–9:

> And the whole earth was of one language, and of one speech. And it came to pass, as they journeyed from the east, that they found a plain in the land of Shinar; and they dwelt there. And they said one to another, Go to, let us make brick, and burn them throughly. And they had brick for stone, and slime had they for mortar. And they said, Go to, let us build us a city and a tower, whose top may reach unto heaven; and let us make us a name, lest we be scattered abroad upon the face of the whole earth. And the LORD came down to see the city and the tower, which the children of men builded. And the LORD said, Behold, the people is one, and they have all one language; and this they begin to do: and now nothing will be restrained from them, which they have imagined to do. Go to, let us go down, and there confound their language,

that they may not understand one another's speech. So the LORD scattered them abroad from thence upon the face of all the earth: and they left off to build the city. Therefore is the name of it called Babel; because the LORD did there confound the language of all the earth: and from thence did the LORD scatter them abroad upon the face of all the earth.

The setting for the building of the Tower of Babel was between the time of the Flood and the birth of Abraham, about 2200 B.C. As the descendants of Noah multiplied, as described in Genesis 10, they began to migrate outward to other lands as God had commanded. But then the people came to the land of Shinar, later called Mesopotamia or Chaldea. This flat plain lies between the Tigris and Euphrates rivers, between Babylon and Baghdad, and extends southward about three hundred miles to the Persian Gulf. Many think of this area as a semi-desert region, but it is actually one of the most fertile lands in the world. The soil is deep and rich, and a network of canals from the Tigris and Euphrates provide water for irrigation. In the spring season, abundant crops of fruits and vegetables stretch as far as the eye can see. This rich land became the economic foundation for Sumer, Chaldea, Assyria, and Babylon.

When the people after the Flood came to this fertile land, they decided to settle there, because it would provide everything they would need. But we read in Genesis 10:25 that it was also during this time, the days of Peleg, that the land mass of the earth was broken up and divided. Scientists contend that the separation of the islands and continents occurred millions of years ago, but according to the Bible, it was only about four thousand years ago. The fear of being scattered over the face of the earth as a result of the dividing of the earth could have motivated the building of the Tower of Babel. The objective was to keep the people in one place by building a tower whose top would reach into the heavens. Some Bible scholars believe the interpretation should be that a tower was to be constructed with heaven at the top. The people of the Chaldean civilization were worshippers of the moon god, Nannar. Altars and sacrificial places of worship were located on top of the ziggurats and temples at Ur, Nineveh, and Babylon.

It is interesting to notice that the Tower of Babel was made of brick with slime for mortar. The slime pits are still prevalent today in Babylon. The slime is a thick oil, or semi-asphalt, the residue of oil seepage that rises to the surface from oil deposits deep in the ground. There are numerous oil fields today in Iraq between Babylon and the Persian Gulf.

The walls of the buildings of Nineveh were made of stone because that great city is in the mountains about two hundred miles north of Baghdad. But on the lower plains of Mesopotamia, there are no stones. The cities of Babylon and Ur were made of brick, which we are told in the Bible was baked thoroughly. Even after four thousand years, these bricks are still solid, much better than bricks made today. Between Baghdad and Babylon there are many brick furnaces today, where bricks are being made for the rebuilding of Babylon. Ancient Babylon was constructed from hundreds of millions of bricks made in the furnaces of Nebuchadnezzar. These furnaces were also used to cremate many of the Jews taken into captivity. While Meshach, Abednego, and Shadrach escaped the furnace, others did not. We read in Jeremiah 29:22: "And of them shall be taken up a curse by all the captivity of Judah which are in Babylon, saying, The LORD make thee like Zedekiah and like Ahab, whom the king of Babylon roasted in the fire." So Hitler was not the first Jew-hater who burned them in furnaces.

In settling this region after the Flood, the people saw the land was not only fertile and abundant in vegetation, but biblical historians have noted that large herds of deer, elk, and antelope found a natural habitat in the area. This food source for predatory beasts resulted in the land between the Tigris and the Euphrates rivers being overrun by lions, tigers, and leopards, which were a constant danger. Therefore we read in Genesis 10:8–10:

> And Cush begat Nimrod: he began to be a mighty one in the earth. He was a mighty hunter before the LORD: wherefore it is said, Even as Nimrod the mighty hunter before the LORD. And the beginning of his kingdom was Babel, and Erech, and Accad, and Calneh, in the land of Shinar.

A conclusion from this scripture is that Nimrod launched hunting expeditions to rid the land of these fierce beasts. Inscriptions and pictorial accounts in brick and stone in the ruins of Nineveh and Babylon reveal that Assyrian and Babylonian kings hunted and killed these wild animals. From Nimrod doubtless came the tradition that kings should also be great hunters. It has been noted by some authorities of the Hebrew text that Genesis 10:9 could also be interpreted: "He was a mighty hunter who stood against the Lord: wherefore it is said, Even as Nimrod the mighty hunter against the Lord." Nimrod used his reputation as the mighty hunter who saved the people to lead them to defy God.

The *Jewish Encyclopedia* says of Nimrod: "He who made all the people rebellious against God."

Josephus wrote:

> Now it was Nimrod who excited them to such an affront and contempt of God. . . . He also gradually changed the government into tyranny, seeing no other way of turning men from the fear of God . . . the multitudes were very ready to follow the determination of Nimrod . . . and they built a tower, neither sparing any pain, nor being in any degree negligent

about the work; and, by reason of the multitude of hands employed in it, it grew very high. . . . The place wherein they built the tower is now called Babylon.

After the confusion of the language spoken at Babel, and the death of Nimrod, the Middle East became ruled by city-states. Hammurabi, called Amraphel in Genesis 14, was king over Shinar and Babylon. Hammurabi is given a notable place in history for a code of laws, but a note in the Pilgrim Bible on Genesis 14:1 states of this early Babylonian king:

> Amraphel . . . is another name for the Hammurabi of ancient history who drew up the first code of laws. His laws were very often unjust, deliberately favoring rich men and oppressing the poor. Though there are many parallels between this code and the law which God gave later to Israel through Moses, there are also many contrasts, and the latter law is far superior.

Hammurabi made an alliance with four other northern city-states and invaded the cities to the south which included Petra, Sodom, and Gomorrah. Lot and his household living at Sodom were taken captive. When Abraham, who at the time had pitched his tents on the plains of Mamre, received the news, he immediately armed his servants, a force of three hundred eighteen men, and gave chase. He caught up with Hammurabi near Damascus and defeated him and his allies. Abraham rescued Lot and his household and recaptured all the spoils of war that had been taken.

The strongest nation to rise up out of the territories ruled by Nimrod to seriously threaten Israel was Assyria. The capital of Assyria was Nineveh on the Tigris River in the old land of Asshur. Nineveh is today called Mosul. When at the ruins of Nineveh, we were impressed by the huge gates to the ancient city as restored by the government of Iraq.

In about 720 B.C. the Assyrians invaded the northern kingdom of Israel, and of the ten tribes that were not killed, they carried approximately twenty-seven thousand Israelis into captivity to Nineveh. To this day, the fate of the Israelites taken to Assyria remains a mystery. According to inscriptions on the ruins of Sennacherib's palace in Nineveh, they must have been treated cruelly, and it is probable that most died in captivity.

When the Assyrian army besieged Jerusalem, King Hezekiah and the people turned to God and prayed for deliverance. According to 2 Kings 19:35–37, God intervened and one hundred eighty-five thousand Assyrian soldiers died outside the walls of Jerusalem. As a result, Sennacherib was forced to return to Nineveh. Afterward, two of his sons assassinated him, and another of his sons became king.

During the time of the Assyrian kingdom, Babylon was a province. We read in 2 Kings 17:24 that Babylonians were among those foreign races that Assyria brought into Israel to replace the Israelites taken into captivity. But soon after the defeat of the Assyrian army at Jerusalem, Babylon began to take a more prominent role in the Middle East. A delegation from Babylon came to Jerusalem to visit Hezekiah. The account of their visit is recorded in 2 Kings 20:14–19:

> Then came Isaiah the prophet unto king Hezekiah, and said unto him, What said these men? and from whence came they unto thee? And Hezekiah said, They are come from a far country, even from Babylon. And he said, What have they seen in thine house? And Hezekiah answered, All the things that are in mine house have they seen: there is nothing among my treasures that I have not shewed them. And Isaiah said unto Hezekiah, Hear the word of the LORD. Behold, the days come, that all that is in thine house, and that which thy fathers have laid up in store unto this day, shall be car

ried into Babylon: nothing shall be left, saith the LORD. And of thy sons that shall issue from thee, which thou shalt beget, shall they take away; and they shall be eunuchs in the palace of the king of Babylon. Then said Hezekiah unto Isaiah, Good is the word of the LORD which thou hast spoken. And he said, Is it not good, if peace and truth be in my days?

Although in the time of Isaiah, Babylon was still only a province in the Assyrian kingdom, the prophet warns Israel to be on guard against it, and in seven chapters of Isaiah, God's sure judgment against this city is pronounced. For example, we read in Isaiah 21:9: "Babylon is fallen, is fallen; and all the graven images of her gods he hath broken unto the ground."

Concerning the decline of Assyria and the rise of Babylon, we quote from *A History of the Middle East* by Sidney Fisher:

> One of the great empires controlling a major part of the Middle East was that of the Assyrians, whose capital was at Nineveh on the upper Tigris in Mesopotamia. Iron weapons, a disciplined army, a tight bureaucracy, and iron battering rams mounted on wheels gave the Semitic Assyrians such an advantage in the seventh century B.C. that Nineveh held sway from Sinai to the Caspian Sea and from the Persian Gulf to the plains of central Asia Minor. However, overextension of the empire and exhausting battles, coupled with luxury, indolence, and unwise taxation, weakened the army and the government so that Nineveh and its palaces and great library were sacked by Iranians in league with another Semitic group which established its capital at Babylon on the Euphrates. Comprising the full Fertile Crescent from Sinai to the Persian Gulf, the new Chaldean Empire won fame from the "hanging gardens," from the Babylonian captivity of the Hebrews, and from such names as Nebuchadnezzar and Belshazzar.

Nebuchadnezzar became king of Babylon in 606 B.C. His first two objectives were to build Babylon into the strongest and most magnificent city on earth, and to conquer all the world. According to 2 Kings 24 and 25, Judah became a province of Babylon, and Nebuchadnezzar made three separate agreements with Jehoakim, Jehoiachin, and Zedekiah. On two separate occasions he sent his army against Jerusalem to enforce his rule, and finally Nebuchadnezzar himself led his army against the city, sacked it, burned the Temple, and carried many of the holy vessels back to Babylon.

Although successful in escaping from Jerusalem, Zedekiah was captured at Jericho. Zedekiah's sons were killed before his eyes, and then he was blinded, leaving him with this terrible memory of the last thing he saw. All of the men of the royal line of David who were not killed were, like Daniel, made eunuchs. This was another attempt by Satan to prevent the birth of the Messiah.

The name of the first Babylon, Babel, means confusion. The name of the first ruler, Nimrod, comes from the word *marad*, which means "he rebelled." Such kings mark the entire course of Babylon's history — confusing the people and rebelling against God.

Therefore, it is no small wonder that Saddam Hussein, the dictator of Iraq, has been described as the most arrogant and dangerous man in the world.

Chapter 12
Babylon's Fall and Decline

Babylon, before Nebuchadnezzar, was built on the west side of the Euphrates. But Nebuchadnezzar almost doubled its size by building a new city on the east bank. The overall size after the addition was fifteen miles square; therefore, we see Babylon again as one of Satan's many counterfeit schemes to deceive the world, because the New Jerusalem will be fifteen hundred miles square.

Babylon could raise an army of two hundred thousand, so it is concluded that the total population was about one million. Around the city was a wall three hundred fifty feet high and eighty-seven feet thick. Outside the inner wall, equally high, was a second wall. The second wall was one-half mile distant from the first wall, and between the two walls there was thirty square miles of fertile soil. In this area fruit trees of every kind bore fruit practically the year round, and the land could also be used to grow vegetables in times of siege. The Euphrates River ran through Babylon, and water was diverted to fill a thirty-foot-wide moat outside the wall to further discourage invaders. With the morning and evening sun, the reflection off the polished bronze gates gave the wide avenues a golden appearance; so in every respect (size, river, and fruit trees) the city was designed to imitate the New Jerusalem.

Nebuchadnezzar died in 561 B.C. Three male members of his family sat upon the throne in succession over a period of six years; all were assassinated. Finally, an in-law, Nabonnedus, a military strong man, took the throne in 555 B.C. But Nabonnedus was a general, and the empire was being challenged from the east, the west, and the south. And so King Nabonnedus invested most of his time fighting enemies out in the provinces while the second and third ruler of the kingdom sat on the throne. For some unknown reason, Nabonnedus spent several years at an oasis in northwest Arabia, probably Petra. Receiving word that the Medes and Persians were besieging Babylon, he led his army to Haran in Syria, his mother's birthplace. A Haranian inscription, found by archaeologists, records Nabonnedus as saying: "But I hide myself afar from my city of Babylon . . . ten years to my city Babylon I went not in."

In 547 B.C., the Medes and Persians crossed the Tigris and began an assault upon the provinces of Babylon, and actually conquered and held much of the territory including Haran. And so, according to a dream Nabonnedus had, as found in the ruins of Haran, he engaged the enemy in Syria rather than returning to help defend Babylon. The dream is as follows:

At the beginning of my reign the gods let me see a dream: in it there stood both Marduk, the Great Lord, and Sin, the light of heaven and earth. Marduk said to me: "Nabonnedus, King of Babylon, bring bricks on your own horse and chariot and build the temple of Elulhul [the moon god] that Sin, the Great Lord, may take up his dwelling there." I replied to Marduk, the chief of the gods, "Barbarian hordes [the Medes], are laying to the very temple you have ordered me to build and their armed might is very great." But Marduk said to me, "The barbarians of whom you spoke, they, and their country, and all the kinds who mark at their side, shall cease to exist." . . . That was the doing of the Great Lord Marduk, whose command cannot be changed.

Nabonnedus was, evidently, given a temporary victory at Haran and did build a temple to Marduk. The temple of Marduk (the same as the Canaanite god Baal) at Babylon has been restored. But the victory over the Medes at Haran was a rather insignificant one as it in no way affected the final outcome of the war. All these ancient writings of Nabonnedus prove that the Book of Daniel is correct — at the time that Belshazzar, Nabonnedus' son (or adopted son), was on the throne, the nation had renounced the God of Daniel and returned to worshipping the false gods and idols of the Babylonians.

According to the book *Babylon* by John Oates, during the reigns of Nabonnedus and Belshazzar, inflation amounted to two hundred percent. The population resented the return to religious oppression and fanaticism. Taxes were increased to support army expenditures and to build the temples of Marduk and Sin. There was a revival of idol worship that existed in the early days of Nebuchadnezzar.

It seems the majority of the people, according to both Grecian and Persian accounts, were overburdened, discouraged, and disillusioned. The setting for Daniel 5:1–4 is the year 539 B.C. while Nabonnedus and the bulk of the Babylonian army was at Haran:

Belshazzar the king made a great feast to a thousand of his lords, and drank wine before the thousand. Belshazzar, whiles he tasted the wine, commanded to bring the golden and silver vessels which his father Nebuchadnezzar had taken out of the temple which was in Jerusalem; that the king, and his princes, his wives, and his concubines, might drink therein. Then they brought the golden vessels that were taken out of the temple of the house of God which was at Jerusalem; and the king, and his princes, his wives, and his concubines, drank in them. They drank wine, and praised the gods of gold, and of silver, of brass, of iron, of wood, and of stone.

The occasion for this gala event ordered by Belshazzar was the New Year Festival. Again quoting from *Babylon* by John Oates:

In 539 B.C. the New Year Festival was celebrated in Babylon, apparently for the first time since Nabonnedus' retirement in Taima; the Persian account ascribes to the Babylonian king various sacrilegious actions during the festival. During the ceremony a plentiful supply of wine was distributed, and to judge from the accounts of Herodotus, Xenophon, and the author of the Book of Daniel, not only were the revels prolonged, but the memory of them remained fresh for many years.

We also quote from the book *Babylonia and Syria* by H. W. F. Saggs:

During the first five days of the festival, various ceremonies of purification and preparation were performed. These culminated in the High Priest taking the King in before Marduk, to whom he surrendered his royal insignia. . . . On the sixth day the image of the god Nabu arrived . . . and entered the temple of his father Marduk. The details of what Marduk and Nabu did during the following days we do not know: in general terms it is likely that they were engaged in decreeing the fate of the city for the following year. . . . The climax of the festival took place on the tenth day. The statues of Marduk, Nabu, and other gods, dressed in sacred gar-

ments adorned in gold, assembled in the great courtyard.
. . . After his victory Marduk and his procession were taken
back to the city in triumph, the populace shouting over and
over again their ritual cries of joy.

During the New Year Festival in Babylon, the king and his
court were celebrating with wine as was the usual custom.
However, this year they drank to their false gods from the
sacred vessels of the Temple. It was their way of showing contempt for the God of Daniel.

The city was under siege and facing an uncertain future,
so Belshazzar was looking forward to the gods of Babylon to
make known the fate of the city. However, the prophecy concerning the future came not from Babylon's gods, but rather
from the God of the Hebrews. A finger appeared in the air and
wrote on the wall, "Mene, Mene, Tekel, Upharsin." We can
readily understand why the king became deathly afraid and
his knees shook.

It was then that the queen suggested that Daniel be brought
in to interpret the writing. Daniel reminded Belshazzar that
his God had humbled Nebuchadnezzar until he acknowledged
Him as the Most High who ruled in the kingdom of men. Daniel
also added:

And thou his son, O Belshazzar, hast not humbled thine
heart, though thou knewest all this; But hast lifted up thyself against the Lord of heaven; and they have brought the
vessels of his house before thee, and thou, and thy lords, thy
wives, and thy concubines, have drunk wine in them; and
thou hast praised the gods of silver, and gold, of brass, iron,
wood, and stone, which see not, nor hear, nor know: and the
God in whose hand thy breath is, and whose are all thy ways,
hast thou not glorified.

— Daniel 5:22-23

Daniel then told Belshazzar the interpretation of the writing on the wall concerning future of the city:

> This is the interpretation of the thing: MENE; God hath numbered thy kingdom, and finished it. TEKEL; Thou art weighed in the balances, and art found wanting. PERES; Thy kingdom is divided, and given to the Medes and Persians.
>
> — Daniel 5:26–28

And we read in verses thirty and thirty-one: "In that night was Belshazzar the king of the Chaldeans slain. And Darius the Median took the kingdom. . . ."

Nabonnedus did march with his army from the east, but it was too late. He was defeated between the Tigris and Euphrates, and his army annihilated. According to Herodotus, the Medes and the Persians diverted the river into a depression near Aqar Quf; the moat around the city was drained, and they marched into Babylon during the festival unopposed. The historian stated:

> As it was, the Persians came upon them by surprise and so took the city. Owing to the vast size of the place, the inhabitants of the central parts, as the residents of Babylon declare, long after the outer portions of the town were taken, knew nothing of what had chanced, but as they were engaged in a festival, continued dancing and reveling until they learnt the capture but too certainly.

According to archaeological evidence in the book *Babylonia and Assyria,* because of discontent and religious oppression in Babylon under Belshazzar, the Medes and Persians had Babylonian traitors inside the city who worked from within to help them swiftly take the city without a fight. Babylon itself suffered no destruction. History and archaeology verify the biblical account of the fall of Babylon to the Medes and the Persians in every detail.

The New Year Festival in Babylon celebrated by Belshazzar occurred when the sun crossed the vernal equinox in the spring. The festival of Babylon in 1987 began when the sun crossed the vernal equinox in the fall on September 22. The stated reason for this festival was to prove that God is wrong and that Babylon has risen once more from the sands of time to erase the writing on the wall that appeared twenty-five hundred years ago.

According to both the biblical and historical records, the change of government in Babylon was an easy one for the Medes and Persians. Most Babylonians actually welcomed the conquerors as deliverers. Taxes were lightened, and trade and commerce thrived. The Jews were given their freedom, and many returned to rebuild Jerusalem and the Temple.

When the Persian king Xerxes launched his war against Greece, many of his troops and supplies were provided by Babylon. However, when he attempted to place a heavier burden on Babylon for the war effort, the Babylonians rebelled and threw the Persians out. But Xerxes besieged the city, overthrew the rebels, and burned the temple of Marduk. However, the fortunes of Babylon turned once more. Quoting from *Babylon* by John Oates:

> In 465 B.C. Xerxes was assassinated and succeeded by his younger son, Artaxerxes, who seems to have held a more sympathetic attitude toward Babylon. To the priests of Marduk he restored their lands and their positions, but it is doubtful whether much of their temple was standing at this time. However, the detailed descriptions of Herodotus show that despite its harsh treatment, the city was far from destroyed.

In 332 B.C. Alexander the Great set out from Macedonia with the intent of defeating the Persian Empire and then conquering the world. His strategy was to first take all the cities from Constantinople to Alexandria to deprive the Persian fleet of its bases. At Assissi on the Mediterranean coast, in what is now southern Turkey, he learned of a trap that had been set for him by the Persians. In a daring maneuver, he marched inland and caught the Persians in their own trap. He then marched southward past Tyre and Sidon to the mouth of the Nile, and doubled back. He made Babylon his eastern capital and took all the land as far as India. In India he met with disaster and lost over half of his army in retreating back to Babylon, where he became ill and died in 323 B.C.

Under the divided Grecian Empire, Antiochus Seleucus established a nearby city with his own name and forced the population of Babylon to move there. Later, Antiochus Epiphanes in 173 B.C. repopulated the city with a small Grecian population, but it did not last. In 24 B.C. Strabo described Babylon as being most empty and desolate. The Jewish population of the area that remained continued to maintain Babylon's identity in a town on the outskirts with a population of fifteen thousand. The apostle Peter was commissioned by Jesus Christ to take the gospel to the Jews, and in A.D. 63 he concluded his first epistle with these words: "The church that is at Babylon, elected together with you, saluteth you; and so doth Marcus my son." Some interpret Babylon to be Rome, but had Peter been in Rome, there is no reason why he should not have said so. Beyond doubt, the apostle was in Babylon.

In A.D. 116 the Roman General Trajan wintered in Babylon during his war against the Parthians, but he reported that the city itself was mostly desolate and empty. Before departing, he offered a sacrifice in the room where Alexander died. In succeeding centuries, the Euphrates River changed its course and buried the city of Nebuchadnezzar under sand before changing its course once more. There ancient Babylon slept until 1899, the beginning of the twentieth century, when Robert Koldewey, on behalf of Germany, began excavations and unearthed the upper portions of the Ishtar Gate, which are now in the Pergamon Museum in Berlin.

Of the coming of Israel's Messiah to establish His Kingdom and rebuild the nation of Israel, we read in Isaiah 48:12, 14, 20:

> Hearken unto me, O Jacob and Israel, my called; I am he; I am the first, I also am the last. . . . All ye, assemble yourselves, and hear; which among them hath declared these things? The LORD hath loved him: he will do his pleasure on Babylon, and his arm shall be on the Chaldeans. . . . Go ye forth of Babylon, flee ye from the Chaldeans, with a voice of singing declare ye, tell this, utter it even to the end of the earth; say ye, The LORD hath redeemed his servant Jacob.

The government of Iraq says that Babylon will live again and defy the judgment of God. But the Bible says that God will do his pleasure on Babylon, and it will never rise again.

Chapter 13
Babylon the Harlot

There are well-meaning and even knowledgeable Bible scholars who contend that all the prophecies relating to Babylon, even those in Revelation, were fulfilled in the Persian, Macedonian, and Hellenistic periods, before the birth of Jesus Christ. But Babylon was not destroyed in a day; it was not wiped off the face of the earth in a fiery judgment within an hour's time; it's name is still remembered; but with the possible exception of Peter, there were no martyrs of Jesus who died in old Babylon. Therefore, we have to look elsewhere, other than the Babylon that Nebuchadnezzar built, for the identity of mystery Babylon of the last days.

We first read Revelation 17:1–7:

And there came one of the seven angels which had the seven vials, and talked with me, saying unto me, Come hither; I will shew unto thee the judgment of the great whore that sitteth upon many waters: With whom the kings of the earth have committed fornication, and the inhabitants of the earth have been made drunk with the wine of her fornication. So he carried me away in the spirit into the wilderness: and I saw a woman sit upon a scarlet coloured beast, full of names of blasphemy, having seven heads and ten horns. And the woman was arrayed in purple and scarlet colour, and decked with gold and precious stones and pearls, having a golden cup in her hand full of abominations and filthiness of her fornication: And upon her forehead was a name written, MYSTERY, BABYLON THE GREAT, THE MOTHER OF HARLOTS AND ABOMINATIONS OF THE EARTH. And I saw the woman drunken with the blood of the saints, and with the blood of the martyrs of Jesus: and when I saw her, I wondered with great admiration. And the angel said unto me, Wherefore didst thou marvel? I will tell thee the mystery of the woman, and of the beast that carrieth her, which hath the seven heads and ten horns.

It is generally agreed by all reputable Bible scholars who have offered a commentary on Revelation 17 that Babylon, the "mother of harlots," is an evil religious system. This conclusion follows the symbolism set forth in Scripture. The church, the Bride of Christ, is referred to as a chaste virgin. Jezebel, the wife of Ahab, was a prime example of degenerate womanhood, and we read in Revelation 2:20: "Notwithstanding I have a few things against thee, because thou sufferest that woman Jezebel, which calleth herself a prophetess, to teach and to seduce my servants to commit fornication, and to eat things sacrificed unto idols."

We notice that the woman is arrayed in purple. Purple is the color of royalty, so the symbolism follows that she is the concubine of kings. She is also adorned in scarlet, and the color of scarlet on a woman is traditionally the identification of prostitutes. The harlot has evidently been rewarded for her services because she is also decked with gold, precious stones, pearls, and has a golden cup in her hand. If you have ever been to the huge cathedrals in Europe, like the ones at Toledo in Spain, the comparative symbolism is striking. In these cathedrals there are billions of dollars worth of gold ornaments and images, and jewels beyond imagination.

Now we notice that the harlot comes riding upon a scarlet-colored beast. Predatory beasts in the Bible are used as symbols of empires, and they still are today — the lion, bear, leopard, etc. The symbolism is again apparent. The political system or the alliance that will ultimately produce the Antichrist will allow the religious system to ride along for the support and pleasure the beast receives. The harlot will play her part in deceiving all the unsaved world to worship the Antichrist as god.

In Revelation 17:7 we notice again the words of the angel: ". . . I will tell thee the mystery of the woman, and of the beast that carrieth her. . . ." After the angel described the political beast, he spoke again to John:

And he saith unto me, The waters which thou sawest, where the whore sitteth, are peoples, and multitudes, and nations, and tongues. And the ten horns which thou sawest upon the beast, these shall hate the whore, and shall make her desolate and naked, and shall eat her flesh, and burn her with fire. For God hath put in their hearts to fulfil his will, and to agree, and give their kingdom unto the beast, until the words of God shall be fulfilled. And the woman which thou sawest is that great city, which reigneth over the kings of the earth.
— Revelation 17:15–18

There is a jingle which goes:

There was a young lady of Niger,
Who smiled as she rode on a tiger;
They returned from the ride
With the lady inside,
And the smile on the face of the tiger.

This little rhyme illustrates the relation of the religious system to the kingdom of Antichrist during the Tribulation period. The system of religion is destroyed by the Antichrist once she has served her purpose. Some believe the city to be Rome of the first century and the religious system that sprang from Rome. However, this is a conclusion and not a prophetic certainty. So there is still a mystery concerning the real identity of both the religious system and the kingdom of ten rulers. But the setting of the prophecy is the Great Tribulation, and during this period of seven years that precede the coming of Jesus Christ to establish His Kingdom on earth, the identity of both the woman and the beast may not be a mystery.

The city of the religious system of Revelation 17 becomes Babylon in Revelation 18. To understand the mystery religion of Babylon, we should first understand that all the gods of the Chaldeans sprang from the legend of Nimrod. In *The Two Babylons,* Alexander Hislop wrote in great detail concerning the evolvement of the religion of Babylon through the founder of Babel. Concerning some of these gods and goddesses, we quote from the book *Babylon* by John Oates:

> The roots of Babylonian religion lie far back in the prehistoric past. Anu . . . who appears as a shadowy figure throughout Mesopotamian history, originally stood at its head. . . . Under various names Ishtar was later to become the most important goddess through Western Asia. . . . In late Babylonian times the title *Bel, Lord,* became synonymous with Marduk, who like Ishtar assimilated to himself various aspects of other gods. A second group of gods consisted of the astral deities, the Sun, the Moon, and the planet Venus. Of these the moon-god Sin was perhaps the most important. . . . Ishtar, goddess of love and war, was, like Shamash, a child of the moon-god. She was Venus, the Morning and Evening Star, and she often was represented riding on her

sacred beast, the lion. . . . Closely associated with Ishtar, but whose rank in the pantheon is obscure, is Tammuz . . . whose death and disappearance it was custom to mourn. Much has been written about Tammuz and the mythology associated with his name on the assumption that he underwent an annual resurrection.

Another principal Babylonian god was Sin, the moon god, whose worship was often accompanied with the lighting of candles. There were many other gods in the Babylonian pantheon, and the religion of Babylon included amulets to ward off evil spirits and sacrifices to the demons. Marduk was the same as Baal of the Canaanites, and Ishtar was the Diana of the Ephesians and the Grecian world. All the gods of Babylon can be traced to the idols and gods of Greece, Rome, Egypt, and the heathen world. Hinduism and Buddhism are much like, in part, the mystery religion of Babylon.

After Nimrod died, according to the Babylonian tradition, his wife Semiramis bore a son whom she named Tammuz. She claimed that Tammuz was Nimrod reborn, the son of the sun god. This was a satanic deception of the promise of the coming Savior in Genesis 3:15: "And I will put enmity between thee and the woman, and between thy seed and her seed; it shall bruise thy head, and thou shalt bruise his heel." The resurrection of Tammuz was, of course, another part of the satanic lie. Semiramis claimed that her son was supernaturally conceived, so the mother was worshipped as well as the child. Many of the Jews in Babylon accepted, at least in part, this satanic religion, and one of the Jewish months is Tammuz. We read in Ezekiel 8:14–15:

Then he brought me to the door of the gate of the Lord's house which was toward the north; and, behold, there sat women weeping for Tammuz. Then said he unto me, Hast

thou seen this, O son of man? turn thee yet again, and thou
shalt see greater abominations than these.

Concerning the spread of the mystery religion of Babylon, we
quote from the book *Babylon Mystery Religion* by Ralph Woodrow:

> The Chinese had a mother goddess called Shingmoo or the
> "Holy Mother." She is pictured with child in arms and rays
> of glory around her head. The ancient Germans worshipped
> the virgin Hertha with child in arms. The Scandinavians
> called her Disa, who was also pictured with child. The Etr-
> uscans called her Nutria, and among the Druids the Virgo-
> Patitura was worshipped as the "Mother of God." In India,
> she was known as Indrani, who also was represented with
> child in arms. The mother goddess was known as Aphrodite
> to the Greeks; Nana, to the Sumerians; and as Venus to her
> devotees in the olden days of Rome, and her child was Jupi-
> ter. . . . In Asia, the mother was known as Cybele and the
> child as Deouis.
>
> "But regardless of her name or place," says one writer,
> "she was the wife of Baal, the virgin queen of heaven, who
> bore fruit although she never conceived." When the chil-
> dren of Israel fell into apostasy, they too were defiled with
> this mother goddess worship. As we read in Judges 2:13:
> "They forsook the Lord, and served Baal and Ashtaroth."
> . . . One of the titles by which the goddess was known
> among them was "the queen of heaven" (Jer. 44:17–19). . . .
> The prophet Jeremiah rebuked them for worshipping her.
> . . . In Ephesus, the great mother was known as Diana. The
> temple dedicated to her in that city was one of the seven
> wonders of the ancient world! Not only at Ephesus, but
> throughout all Asia and the world was the goddess wor-
> shipped (Acts 19:27). In Egypt, the mother was known as

Isis and her child as Horus. . . . This false worship, having spread from Babylon to the various nations, in different names and forms, finally became established at Rome and throughout the Roman Empire.

It should also be noted that many of the idols of Diana by the idol makers at Ephesus were made with a replica of the Tower of Babel on top of her head, recognizing the false religion of Babylon and that the goddess was actually the wife of Nimrod. The worship of the pseudo-goddess and her offspring in all nations can be traced back to Babel and the incorporation of this satanic deception into the mystery religion of Babylon. Israel and Judah were warned repeatedly by the prophets of God to reject this prostitution by the Devil of the promise of a coming Redeemer, but they continued to follow the false prophets of Baal under Jezebel. Finally, God allowed them first to be subjugated by Assyria and then by Babylon from whence the religion came.

Isaiah repeatedly warned Israel against worshipping the gods and goddesses of Babylon, but then the prophet pointed to the birth of the true Savior of God: ". . . Hear ye now, O house of David; Is it a small thing for you to weary men, but will ye weary my God also? Therefore the Lord himself shall give you a sign; Behold, a virgin shall conceive, and bear a son, and shall call his name Immanuel" (Isa. 7:13–14).

In the fullness of time a virgin by the name of Mary did conceive and bear a Son by the Holy Ghost. Certainly Mary was a handmaiden of the Lord, especially chosen according to time, circumstances, and heritage to bring the Savior into the world to save sinners. She is to be called blessed by all who receive Jesus Christ as Lord and Savior. But there is no scripture in all the Bible that even implies that her birth was of a divine nature, that she was sinless, that she was caught up to heaven, or that she is to be worshipped or prayed to by Christians. None of the apostles or disciples worshipped her or directed intercessions before God to her. There is not one single word of evidence in the records of the early church that Mary was worshipped or considered more than being the mother of the Lord. "For there is one God, and one mediator between God and men, the man Christ Jesus; Who gave himself a ransom for all, to be testified in due time" (1 Tim. 2:5–6).

The *Encyclopaedia Britannica* states that in the Christian churches of the first centuries, no emphasis was placed upon the worship of Mary. The *Catholic Encyclopedia* reports:

> Devotion to our Blessed Lady in its ultimate analysis must be regarded as a practical application of the doctrine of the Communion of Saints. Seeing that this doctrine is not contained, at least explicitly, in the earlier forms of the Apostles' Creed, there is perhaps no ground for surprise if we do not meet with any clear traces of the cults of the Blessed Virgin in the first Christian centuries.

It was not until Emperor Constantine made Christianity the state religion of the Roman Empire that Mariology became an important part of church doctrine. Because of the Babylonish religion that had spread to all the world, it became easier for the heathen world to profess allegiance to the state church if the main beliefs in the traditions of Nimrod could be incorporated into worship. In A.D. 431 at the Council of Ephesus, the worship of Mary in the form that is prevalent today was adopted as an official church doctrine.

In the book *Babylon Mystery Religion,* the author states:

> A further indication that Mary worship developed out of the old worship of the mother goddess may be seen in the titles by which the Babylonian goddess was known. In deified form, Nimrod came to be known as Baal. The title of his wife, the

female divinity, would be in the equivalent of Baalti. In English, the word means "My Lady"; in Latin, "Mea Domina"; and in Italian, it is corrupted into the well-known "Madonna"!

Therefore, it is no mystery that the government of Iraq has stated that the rock star Madonna of the United States lives in the heart of the Iraqi people, and why she was invited to reign as queen over the Festival of Babylon in 1987.

Chapter 14
Babylon in the Church

In our previous chapter we discussed the attempt by Satan to counterfeit the promise of God to send the seed of woman to bruise the serpent's head. This deception came first before the Flood when Satan attempted to defile the entire human race through fallen angelic corruption. After the Flood, Satan diverted the attention of mankind from the coming Savior through the rise of the false religion, Mystery Babylon. As we have already noted, the base of this satanic counterfeit salvation was the myth that after Nimrod's death his wife gave birth to a son whom she named Tammuz. The worship of Nimrod's wife, Semiramis, as the queen of heaven, along with her god-son, spread throughout the world. It exists today in many forms, even within Christendom.

A tradition related to the religion of Babylon is that when Nimrod died, his body was cut into pieces, cremated, and the ashes were spread over the earth. In Judges 19 we find what may be considered a comparative story about a concubine who went out from her master and became a whore. Her flesh and bones were cut into many pieces and scattered throughout the coasts of Israel. The origin of such heathenish practices was probably in the scattering of Nimrod's human parts, and may illustrate the dissemination of the religion of Babylon into all the world.

In the case of Nimrod, according to the tradition as related by some ancient sources, all of the body was cut up and scattered with the exception of his reproductive organs. It was from this ancient and obscure Babylonian tradition that the worship of the "phallus" began.

In Genesis 10 we read that Ham begat Cush, and Cush begat Nimrod. It is generally agreed by most Bible scholars that Nimrod was a black man. The next great king of Babylon to arise after Nimrod was Hammurabi, his name signifying that he was a descendant of Nimrod through Ham. The laws of Hammurabi were graven on a large black stone in the shape of a phallus.

In Egypt, Semiramis took the name of Isis, and Tammuz became Horus. The *Encyclopedia of Religions* (vol. 3, p. 264) states that Queen Semiramis in Babylon erected an obelisk one hundred thirty feet high to the memory of Nimrod. Such temples were common in Babylon and later in Egypt. These obelisks are replete in the temples of Luxor and Karnak. Many of the monuments have been removed to other nations. One stands in Central Park in New York City, one in London, and others in Italy.

According to *The Two Babylons* by Hislop and *Babylon Mystery Religion* by Woodrow, these obelisks, or standing images as they were called in the Hebrew, are mentioned in both 1 and 2 Kings as a part of Baal worship. Baal is one of the names for Nimrod. It was into this kind of evil and licentious religion that Jezebel enticed Israel. It is to the abolition of the last vestiges of the Babylonian idolatry that Isaiah 27:1 and 9 is addressed:

> In that day the LORD with his sore and great and strong sword shall punish leviathan the piercing serpent, even leviathan

that crooked serpent; and he shall slay the dragon that is in the sea. . . . By this therefore shall the iniquity of Jacob be purged; and this is all the fruit to take away his sin; when he maketh all the stones of the altar as chalkstones that are beaten in sunder, the groves and images shall not stand up.

A common practice in Egypt, Greece, and other nations of the Middle East and the Mediterranean area, where the religion of Babylon had spread was to erect an obelisk in front of the temple. This symbolism for the phallus associated the religion with the fertility cult of Nimrod. The temples of Diana, the Ephesian counterpart of Nimrod's wife, the queen of heaven, was supported by the temple prostitutes. According to Ezekiel 8:1–6, this abominable symbol was erected in front of the temple at the north gate. Ezekiel referred to it as the "image of jealousy." We can be certain that it was the Babylonian symbol of Nimrod because we read in verse fourteen that the prophet saw a woman at the temple weeping for Tammuz, the son of Nimrod.

Emperor Caligula was one of the most cruel and degenerate of the Caesars of Rome. According to the book *Babylon Mystery Religion*, Caligula transported an obelisk from Heliopolis in Egypt to the section of Rome which is called his *circus*. This hill is the place where the Vatican was later built. The obelisk remained in the Vatican until 1586 when Pope Sixtus V had it moved in front of the church at St. Peter's Square where it is today. The pope had decreed the death penalty if it should be broken or damaged. The mover was a man named Domenico Fontana. Forty-five winches, one hundred sixty horses, and a crew of eight hundred men were required to move the obelisk to its new location. When the task was completed, the pope blessed it and the workmen who had moved it under such an extreme penalty for failure. An inscription in the pagan temple of Heliopolis, from where the obelisk came, reads: "I, Dionysus, dedicated these phalli to Hera, my stepmother." The account of the moving of the obelisk can be found in the Hastings *Encyclopedia of Religion and Ethics,* in a section on "phallicism."

It is also interesting to take note that the obelisk in front of St. Peter's Cathedral came from Heliopolis. We read in Jeremiah 43:13: "He shall break also the images of Bethshemesh, that is in the land of Egypt; and the houses of the gods of the Egyptians shall he burn with fire." The footnote in the Pilgrim Bible on Bethshemesh reads: "This means 'House of the Sun,' or temples dedicated to sun-worship. . . . This was probably the city which was called Heliopolis by the Greeks."

Wherever we have gone in the world, we have seen the obelisk in its relationship to the mystery religion of Babylon. In China we saw the entire land punctuated with Buddhist shrines called *pagodas.* These pagodas rise high in the sky in tiers, much like the Tower of Babel and the phallus symbol of Nimrod. In China, Semiramis, the mother goddess, was called Shingmoo. Throughout the Moslem world from Morocco to Egypt, to Syria, Jordan, and Iraq, we have seen mosques surrounded by minarets, slender spires with an enlarged section at the top. The symbolism is apparent. Mecca, in the heart of Islam, fractures the skyline with a host of minarets with their slight enlargements at the apex.

In the fourth and fifth centuries, the Roman Empire divided into two parts, with Constantinople becoming the capital city of the eastern leg. The church at St. Sophia was the pride of the holy Byzantine Empire. In front of St. Sophia in the town square was erected a tall obelisk. This obelisk is still standing today. When we were in Istanbul, our guide informed us that it was at this obelisk where doctrinal disagreements were settled through athletic contests. After the Turks captured Constantinople in 1292 and changed the name to Istanbul, St. Sophia was converted to a mosque and minarets were erected around it.

In temples, shrines, mosques, and churches of all religions of the world, obelisk-like spires and towers are included in construction. Many of these elongated units simply follow tradition without any realization of their meaning or relationship to the mystery religion of Babylon.

The obelisk in front of St. Peter's in Rome, including the foundation, is one hundred thirty-two feet high. Inasmuch as it came from Heliopolis in Egypt, it is probably no coincidence that it is approximately the same height as the one that Queen Semiramis erected in honor of her husband, Nimrod. But the largest obelisk in the world is in front of our nation's capitol building in Washington, D.C., the Washington Monument. Again, it was probably no coincidence that the phallus-shaped obelisk was chosen to memorialize George Washington as the father of the United States. We will comment on its relationship to Mystery Babylon later in this study.

As we consider the major religions of mankind, there are literally hundreds of connections that could be made to the mystery religion of Babylon. The most prominent, besides the obelisk, is the worship of idols, or the use of idols in worship.

As evil as the thoughts and deeds of mankind became in the millennium before the Flood, there is no evidence that idol worship was among its sins. Idol worship originated at Babel, and after Babel as the people were scattered over the face of the earth, they carried with them this religious abomination. Throughout Egypt, the Hebrews were confronted with idols to the Egyptian gods, which in reality were only Babylonian gods that had been given Egyptian names. When they passed through the lands of the Canaanite tribes, they saw similar idols which had been given Canaanite names. Therefore, the Lord gave this commandment to Moses for the Israelites: "Ye shall make you no idols nor graven image, neither rear you up a standing image, neither shall ye set up any image of stone in your land, to bow down unto it: for I am the LORD your God." (Lev. 26:1).

The Babylonian concept of idol worship was the chief weapon of Satan that the prophets of God had to contend with. There are thousands of references in the Old Testament alone to idol worship. Like a large segment of both Catholic and non-Catholic Christendom today, the Hebrews tried to make a pretense of worshipping God while catering to their idolatry. We read in Jeremiah 7:8–10, 18, 30–31:

> Behold, ye trust in lying words, that cannot profit. Will ye steal, murder, and commit adultery, and swear falsely, and burn incense unto Baal, and walk after other gods whom ye know not; And come and stand before me in this house, which is called by my name, and say, We are delivered to do all these abominations? . . . The children gather wood, and the fathers kindle the fire, and the women knead their dough, to make cakes to the queen of heaven, and to pour out drink offerings unto other gods, that they may provoke me to anger. . . . For the children of Judah have done evil in my sight, saith the LORD: they have set their abominations in the house which is called by my name, to pollute it. And they have built the high places of Tophet, which is in the valley of the son of Hinnom, to burn their sons and their daughters in the fire; which I commanded them not, neither came it into my heart.

It was the worship of idols, mainly Baal (Nimrod) and the queen of heaven (Nimrod's wife) that brought the judgment of God upon the nation. In the early church it was idol worshippers and makers at Ephesus and other cities who were the fiercest enemies of the disciples. In Athens, the city was overrun with idols, so much so that they even had an idol to the unknown god! In Rome, at the Pantheon, there were idols to every god in the known world.

Like the Israelites, there were some in the early church who professed Jesus Christ as Lord and Savior, yet clung to their heathen idols. We read of this abomination in 2 Corinthians 6:15–17:

> And what concord hath Christ with Belial? or what part hath he that believeth with an infidel? And what agreement hath the temple of God with idols? for ye are the temple of the living God; as God hath said, I will dwell in them, and walk in them; and I will be their God, and they shall be my people. Wherefore come out from among them, and be ye separate, saith the Lord, and touch not the unclean thing; and I will receive you.

In India, the Hindu temples are filled with idols of the Babylonian fertility cult; in Bangkok, the temples are likewise filled with idols; in China, the Buddhist temples have the largest idols in the world. After the Council of Ephesus in A.D. 431 sanctioned the worship of the god-mother religion, the churches of Asia became filled with idols. When Mohammed ravaged the churches of this territory early in the seventh century, he brought fifteen hundred idols back to Mecca. Regardless how identifiable statues are with Christianity, it is an abomination to worship and kiss them. We read in 1 Kings 19:18: ". . . I have left me seven thousand in Israel, all the knees which have not bowed unto Baal, and every mouth which hath not kissed him." Kissing an idol is associated with the worship of Baal, or Nimrod.

All idol worship is related to the mystery religion of Babylon, and all religions are invested with it to some degree. The time is coming when the world religion of the Tribulation, Mystery Babylon, will call upon all idol worshippers on earth to worship one idol, the image of Antichrist: "And he had power to give life unto the image of the beast, that the image of the beast should both speak, and cause that as many as would not worship the image of the beast should be killed" (Rev. 13:15).

The religion of Babel was centered in the person of Nimrod. This religion was to weld a one-world worship in rebellion against God. After Babel this fractured religion was carried into all the world where it has been propagated and perpetuated in various forms. However, its stronghold was retained in Babylon. It would appear that at the fall of Babylon God placed barriers upon this satanic deception and his fallen angels to prevent it from corrupting the entire world. But according to the prophetic Word of God, at the end of the age fractured Babylonianism would unite once more to produce another world leader who would defy God and declare to the whole world that he is god. This we see taking place today. We read in Revelation 9:13–15:

> And the sixth angel sounded, and I heard a voice from the four horns of the golden altar which is before God, Saying to the sixth angel which had the trumpet, Loose the four angels which are bound in the great river Euphrates. And the four angels were loosed, which were prepared for an hour, and a day, and a month, and a year, for to slay the third part of men.

This prophetic warning is repeated in Revelation 16:12–14:

> And the sixth angel poured out his vial upon the great river Euphrates; and the water thereof was dried up, that the way of the kings of the east might be prepared. And I saw three unclean spirits like frogs come out of the mouth of the dragon, and out of the mouth of the beast, and out of the mouth of the false prophet. For they are the spirits of devils, work-

ing miracles, which go forth unto the kings of the earth and of the whole world, to gather them to the battle of that great day of God Almighty.

The confusion within Christendom today, the rise of Eastern religions in our own nation, and the rapid growth of the New Age movement indicate that mankind is rapidly approaching the Great Tribulation and Jesus Christ will come as a thief for those who are not watching.

The major religions of mankind today are looking for a messiah to come. The New Age religion adherents are predicting that Maitreya will come; messianic fervor is now sweeping Israel; a large segment of the Islamic nations wait for Mahdi. This, too, is a sign that Jesus Christ, the true Messiah, may appear at any time (Matt. 24:23–27).

Chapter 15

The Babylonian Priesthood

As we continue our study of the Mystery Babylon of the last days, we take particular notice of the relationship of the religious system, called the Great Whore, to the political empire of Antichrist and the kings of the earth. We read in Revelation 14:8–10:

> And there followed another angel, saying, Babylon is fallen, is fallen, that great city, because she made all nations drink of the wine of the wrath of her fornication. And the third angel followed them, saying with a loud voice, If any man worship the beast and his image, and receive his mark in his forehead, or in his hand, The same shall drink of the wine of the wrath of God, which is poured out without mixture into the cup of his indignation; and he shall be tormented with fire and brimstone in the presence of the holy angels, and in the presence of the Lamb.

In Revelation 17 the "mother of harlots" is depicted riding on the back of the political beast, and in Revelation 18:3 we read that the kings of the earth commit fornication with her.

Nimrod, the father of Babylon, was not only the king of Babel, he was also a high priest. And from Nimrod came a priesthood that directed the worship of the people to the king of the empire as a god. The priesthood of Nimrod was carried on in various nations and religions in many forms and functions. In Buddhism and Hinduism, the prevalent religions of the East, a succession of priests to intercede between the people and the gods have continued to this day. In the early church there were those who attempted to establish the authority of such a priesthood over the churches, and it was these false priests to whom Revelation 2:6 is addressed: "But this thou hast, that thou hatest the deeds of the Nicolaitanes, which I also hate."

In the year 63 B.C., Julius Caesar was given the official title of "Pontifex Maximus," meaning the high priest. The Caesars were not the only high priests over the Babylonish religious system of the Roman Empire; they were, like Nimrod, hailed as gods. Like Nimrod, each was the high priest, god, and king. This was a satanic corruption of the position of Jesus Christ within the Godhead. As our High Priest, He is God, and He is King of kings. There is a Roman coin of the first century B.C. which shows Augustus Caesar with the title "Ponti-Max."

The priesthood of Israel, with the high priest at the head, was established by God through Aaron. All the offices within this priesthood, and its functions, were for the purpose of directing the worship of Israel to God, to intercede between them and God, and to offer up animal sacrifices for sin until the Messiah came and offered up one sacrifice for sin for all. If there is one nation, or one religion, on the face of the earth with reason to establish and carry on such a priesthood, it is Israel under Judaism today. But we find no such priesthood or high priest in Israel. Why? Because when Jesus Christ came and died on the cross, and the Temple was subsequently destroyed, that priesthood was abolished. We read in Hebrews 9:11–14:

> But Christ being come an high priest of good things to come,
> by a greater and more perfect tabernacle, not made with
> hands, that is to say, not of this building; Neither by the
> blood of goats and calves, but by his own blood he entered in
> once into the holy place, having obtained eternal redemp-
> tion for us. For if the blood of bulls and of goats, and the
> ashes of an heifer sprinkling the unclean, sanctifieth to the
> purifying of the flesh: How much more shall the blood of
> Christ, who through the eternal Spirit offered himself with-
> out spot to God, purge your conscience from dead works to
> serve the living God?

The Christian does not need a confessor to purge his con-
science, or a mediator between him and God. We read in 1 Tim-
othy 2:5–6: " For there is one God, and one mediator between
God and men, the man Christ Jesus; Who gave himself a ransom for all, to be testified in due time."

The Roman emperors continued to hold the spiritual office of the Supreme Pontiff until Gratian refused it in A.D. 376.
He believed the position to be idolatrous and un-Christian.
So, in A.D. 378 Demasus, bishop of Rome, was given the title of
Pontifex Maximus. Thereafter, within Christendom the office
of a high priest, with a lower caste of supporting priesthood,
was established. This system has been carried on in various
branches of Christianity to this day. But such a religious system has no scriptural foundation. It is more Babylonish in
origin and tradition than Christian. In fact, the garments of
the high priests and the order of priesthood are very similar
to those of the religion of Babylon.

Supposedly, the basis for the office of a high priest within
Christendom is the tradition that Simon Peter established
when he went to Rome. However, there is absolutely no scriptural evidence that Peter was ever in Rome. Peter was sent as
an apostle to the Jews, while Paul was sent to the Gentiles.

Considerable evidence has been presented that the Simon who was in Rome was actually Simon the sorcerer of Acts 8. The *Catholic Encyclopedia* states of this Simon:

> Justin Martyr and other early writers inform us that he afterward went to Rome, worked miracles there by the power of demons, and received divine honors both in Rome and in his own country. Though much extravagant legend afterward gathered around the name of this Simon . . . it seems nevertheless probable that there must be some foundation in fact for the account given by Justin and accepted by Eusebius. The historical Simon Magus no doubt founded some sort of religion as a counterfeit of Christianity in which he claimed to play a part analogous to that of Christ.

After the office of Pontifex Maximus was vacated by Gratian, it became strictly a religious position within Christendom. Nevertheless, under the doctrine of Divine Right of Kings, no ruler or king of Europe could be crowned without the blessing and coronation by this supreme religious authority. The intrigue and power struggle between the crowned heads of Europe and the central religious authority in Rome are well recorded in European history.

In the year A.D. 800, Pope Leo III crowned Charlemagne emperor of Rome and gave him the holy mission of unifying all Christendom under the authority of the church. With the decline and fall of the Roman Empire, over the next four centuries this authority was transferred to Germany. According to Edward Crankshaw, author of *The Fall of the House of Hapsburg,* this divine duty was conferred upon Rudolf, Count of Hapsburg, the emperor of the Germans, in A.D. 1283. Again, the wars and efforts of the Hapsburgs to weld a Holy Roman Empire of Europe are history.

A contemporary successor to Count Rudolf Hapsburg is

Otto Von Hapsburg, a member of the Common Market Parliament, who made the following observation in 1984:

> If Iran collapses in its war with Iraq, there will be a chain reaction all through the Middle East. . . . The Shiites believe that the twelfth Imman (successor to Mohammed) is coming back. They believe this Mahdi — their messiah — is about to approach, that there will be a united world directed by the Shiites, that Khomeini is the prophet of the approaching Mahdi. . . . Europe too has a right to be decolonized. That is our responsibility toward those of Eastern Europe. . . . It is our duty to see to it that one day they shall have an opportunity to exercise their right of self-determination (in the European Parliament). . . . This is the reason we must strive for a political Europe. . . . Back in the events of politics is still a moral and mental attitude. The religious foundation of a society is the only real and lasting foundation that this society may have . . . to return truly and fully again to the roots of our greatness. . . . We are already in a political Europe. . . . We are well beyond the point of no return. . . . We have not yet arrived at the other shore; but we can't go back.

The return of Europe to the religious roots of its greatness could only refer to the concept of the unification of a political Europe, the revived Roman Empire under a single religious authority. The first major breakdown in papal authority over the kings of Europe came in 1527 when King Henry VIII of England was successful in terminating the authority of Rome over the British throne. The aftermath of the Protestant Reformation further weakened the ties between the royal families of Europe and Rome. However, though somewhat dormant, the ambition to exercise religious dictation to the kings of the earth has remained a cherished goal. Today, each of over one hundred nations, including the United States, has an ambassador to the Vatican. We have presented this information as a possible explanation of the religious system called Mystery Babylon in Revelation. But as we also read in Revelation, after the system has worked to bring all the false religions of the world to worship the Antichrist as god, it will be destroyed:

> And the ten horns which thou sawest upon the beast, these shall hate the whore, and shall make her desolate and naked, and shall eat her flesh, and burn her with fire. For God hath put in their hearts to fulfil his will, and to agree, and give their kingdom unto the beast, until the words of God shall be fulfilled. And the woman which thou sawest is that great city, which reigneth over the kings of the earth.
>
> — Revelation 17:16–18

We are in no way stating that the Babylonish system of religion is centered in one specific church or faith. However, it is consolidated in some more than others. At the beginning of Babel the religious system was to serve Nimrod the king. In the city of Babylon the same was true. In Daniel 2 we find that Nebuchadnezzar demanded that the Chaldean priesthood and the leaders of the occult reveal to him a dream that he had dreamed. When they failed, he decreed that they all be killed. In Babylon, the king was head of everything, including the birds of the air and the beasts of the field.

The image the king saw in his dream represented the "times of the Gentiles." This period extended from the reign of Nebuchadnezzar to the coming of the Messiah to set up an everlasting kingdom. Babylon was the first Gentile kingdom. Daniel pointed to Nebuchadnezzar and said, "Thou art this head of gold." The head controls the rest of the body, and the Babylonish system will determine the course of Gentile empires until a king, like Nebuchadnezzar, will gain power over all nations, peoples, commerce, wealth, and everything that lives. We read in Revelation 13:7–9:

> And it was given unto him to make war with the saints, and to overcome them: and power was given him over all kindreds, and tongues, and nations. And all that dwell upon the earth shall worship him, whose names are not written in the book of life of the Lamb slain from the foundation of the world. If any man have an ear, let him hear.

It would appear the religious system of the last Babylon is also in view in Revelation 18:7–8:

> How much she hath glorified herself, and lived deliciously, so much torment and sorrow give her: for she saith in her heart, I sit a queen, and am no widow, and shall see no sorrow. Therefore shall her plagues come in one day, death, and mourning, and famine; and she shall be utterly burned with fire: for strong is the Lord God who judgeth her.

It is our understanding of Scripture that the true church, the Bride of Christ, will be taken out of the world at the beginning of the Tribulation period. Mystery Babylon, the mother of harlots, will be left waiting at the altar. But she attaches herself to another love, the Antichrist, and boasts that she is no widow — she reigns as a queen of the beast empire. She assumes the position of Semiramis, the queen of heaven. As the saints of the Tribulation are killed for not worshipping the Antichrist and receiving his mark, she thinks that no such sorrow will come to her. But suddenly, even as Nebuchadnezzar almost destroyed the religious system of Babylon in his day, a decree comes from the Antichrist for the kings of his empire to destroy every vestige of the religious element.

In his book *Hidden Prophecies in the Psalms,* Rev. J. R.

Church developed a pattern of prophecies that have been fulfilled in the twentieth century. Beginning with Psalm 1 he shows how a prophecy in that psalm was fulfilled in the year 1901. He then continues psalm by psalm, and we notice that Babylon is mentioned in Psalm 87:1–4:

> His foundation is in the holy mountains. The LORD loveth the gates of Zion more than all the dwellings of Jacob. Glorious things are spoken of thee, O city of God. Selah. I will make mention of Rahab and Babylon to them that know me: behold Philistia, and Tyre, with Ethiopia; this man was born there.

God loves Jerusalem, the city of Zion, more than all the cities of the world where Jacob is still scattered today. And as the psalm indicates, the major concern of Israel today is the growing population of the Arab-Palestinians who are clamoring for independent status. Tyre, which is in Lebanon, is still a major problem to the state of Israel. Ethiopia to the south of Israel refers to the threat of the invasion of Russia with an alliance of nations that surround Israel — Libya, Iran, and Ethiopia. The psalmist wrote: "I will make mention of Rahab and Babylon to them that know me."

Rev. Church says of this passage in Psalm 87:

> The psalmist referred to Rahab, a notorious harlot in the days of Joshua, connecting her with the mystery religion of ancient Babylon. It seems that God has thus promised to reveal the harlot Babylon to those who desire to know the mystery. The Apostle John called her MYSTERY, BABYLON THE GREAT, THE MOTHER OF HARLOTS AND ABOMINATIONS OF THE EARTH (Rev. 17:5). To this day, BABYLON THE GREAT has remained a mystery. Perhaps soon, however, she will be revealed.

When Rev. Church wrote his commentary on Psalm 87, the month-long festival in Babylon — to let the world know that the city lives again — had not been announced. This event, of course, adds new meaning to this psalm. It is also interesting that we read in Psalm 89:10, "Thou hast broken Rahab in pieces, as one that is slain. . . ." The breaking of Rahab in pieces could refer to the judgment mentioned in Revelation that is determined for Babylon in the last days.

Chapter 16
U.S.A. and Babylon

Dr. S. Franklin Logsdon in the first half of this book states:

This Babylonian matter is comprehended within three designations: (1) *Historical Babylon* in Genesis 11; (2) *Ecclesiastical Babylon* in Revelation 17; and (3) *Political Babylon* in Revelation 18. Historical Babylon will ultimately manifest itself in two imposing branches, viz., the false church and a powerful God-forsaking nation. . . .

Historical Babylon is symbolized by a monumental tower, *ecclesiastical Babylon* by a mystical woman, and *political Babylon* by a mighty city. The aim is, respectively, to reach heaven, to rob heaven, and to reject heaven. The proposal of the first was a common language. The proposal of the second is a common worship. The proposal of the third is a common privilege — one speech, one church, one society. . . .

In the case of historical Babylon, God felled the tower, confounded the tongues, and scattered the people.

In the case of ecclesiastical or religious Babylon, the beast (Antichrist) will hate the "harlot" (meaning the false church), outlaw religion, and finally kill the "woman"; that is, he will destroy the final development of organized religion.

In the case of prophesied political Babylon, trials will plague the earth, the economy will crash, the great city will be made desolate. . . .

Babylonism is not only a system of contradictory works, but a scheme of unmitigated robbery, depriving the infinite God of the praise and glory due His holy name, denying His power and His operations. . . .

God, who established His battalions in the skies, from before the foundation of the world, has set the exact time for each of His inevitable victories of these forces of unrighteousness. He will eliminate utterly the false church through the agency of Antichrist or the coming world dictator (Rev. 17:17). He will also completely destroy a powerful end-time nation which is spiritually called Babylon (Rev. 18:18). The word "end-time" connotes the closing days of the present order of things.

Many other prophetic observers, like Dr. Logsdon, see in the destruction of Babylon at the end of the age a mystery religion, a mystery economic system, a mystery city, and a mystery nation. And, Dr. Logsdon and others have reached the conclusion that the mystery nation is the United States. As objectionable and unpatriotic as this presumption may appear to us, this viewpoint is worthy of careful consideration.

That God loves America is not the point in question here. Our nation was founded on a strong biblical foundation. Our first settlers came here to find a land where they could worship God in spirit and in truth. God is recognized in our supreme law of the land, our Constitution; we have given a home to the homeless; churches dot the landscape in every city; we have sent Christian missionaries to all nations; and the United States has been a refuge for God's earthly people, the Jews. We fully believe that God does love America, but God also loved Israel. The biblical precept is: To whom much is given, much is required.

During the coming Great Tribulation, the Antichrist will be the ruler of all nations, none excepted. We read in Micah 5:15: "And I will execute vengeance in anger and fury upon the heathen. . . ." We read also in Ezekiel 39:21: ". . . all the heathen shall see my judgment. . . ." Likewise, Obadiah 15: "For the day of the LORD is near upon all the heathen. . . ." And Revelation 19:15: "And out of his mouth goeth a sharp sword, that with it he should smite the nations. . . ." Without doubt, the United States will be a partaker in the destructive judgments that will come upon all nations in the last days.

Going back to the foundations of Babylon, the primary reason for the building of the Tower of Babel was to build a tower with a top to reach into heaven. The two nations that have opened a gateway to the heavens through a space program are Russia and the United States, but it is significant that the United States has been the only nation to send human beings to another heavenly body — the moon.

According to the prophetic description of the nation of Babylon in the end-time, that nation will be identified by a great city. According to the *2000 World Almanac,* New York City, consisting of five boroughs, is one of the largest cities in the world, with a population of 16,332,000. New York City is allegorically called "the Babylon on the Hudson." On Long Island, across from mainland New York City, is Babylon, New York, zip code 11702, with a population of 12,249 in 1998. At the entrance to New York City is our most emblematic national monument, the Statue of Liberty. Irregardless of the spiritual significance we, and the rest of the world, may subscribe to the Statue of Liberty, it is interesting to note that it is approximately the same height as the obelisk in front of St. Peter's Basilica. The Statue of Liberty is one hundred eleven feet high. In 1986 a rededication of the Statue of Liberty took place; the rededication of Babylon occurred in 1987. The rededication of the Statue of Liberty, accompanied by one of the most elaborate celebrations the United States has ever witnessed, fell one year short of the massive celebration for the revival of Babylon.

We have previously commented in some detail concerning the identification of the obelisk with the worship of Nimrod and the mystery Babylon religious system. According to Ralph Woodrow, as stated in *Babylon Mystery Religion,* two of the highest obelisk structures in the world are the tower of the great Cathedral of Cologne, which is five hundred twelve feet high, and the tower of the Cathedral of Ulm, which is five hundred twenty-eight feet high — both in Germany. However, the tallest obelisk in all the world is on a small hill in front of our nation's capitol building, the Washington Monument, which is five hundred fifty-five and a half feet tall. This national monument was built in honor of the father of our country, George Washington. The Washington Monument is open to the public three hundred sixty-four days a year; the only day it is closed is Christmas Day, the day when Christians remember the birth of Jesus Christ.

Many of the prophecies in the Bible have double meanings. We notice this fact especially in Isaiah where most prophecies about the coming Messiah refer to His first coming as Savior to offer Himself as an offering for sin, and then again to His second coming to establish His kingdom on earth. Jeremiah 50 and 51 relate to God's judgment of Babylon. Some of the verses in these chapters refer to the Babylon of Jeremiah's day, while others refer to the final destruction of Babylon. They could not all refer to the Babylon of the sixth century B.C., because the sudden and ultimate destruction as foretold by Jeremiah is in the day of the Lord's vengeance upon the earth, and in the day when Israel will return from all nations seeking the Lord their God.

We read in Jeremiah 50:37, "A sword is upon . . . the mingled people that are in the midst of her. . . ." It was at Babel that God confounded the language of mankind and scattered the people over the face of the earth. At Babylon, Nebuchadnezzar sought to reverse God's decree for the division of races and nations. In each race, there are distinctive skills and abilities inherent to a particular nation or race. At Babylon the young scientists from Judah were among those brought to the country, and those having particular skills, talents, and aptitudes from all nations were congregated once more to incorporate collective knowledge in building a kingdom that Nebuchadnezzar thought would endure forever. Quoting from *Everyday Life in Babylonia and Assyria:*

> The population of Babylon was a very mixed one, both racially and socially. As to race, Nebuchadnezzar impressed labour gangs for his public works in Babylon from the whole of his empire. Many of these were no doubt only too glad to return to their native lands . . . but others certainly stayed for good in Babylon, either settling down with wives who had followed them from their homeland or marrying local women. Such foreign settlers were no more than the most recent importation of foreign blood. There were many other peoples who during the preceding centuries had been in the city, whether as conquerors, captives, or just visitors, long enough to interbreed with Babylonian ladies. Amongst these were Cassites, Hittites, Elamites, and an occasional Egyptian, Arameans, Assyrians, Chaldeans, and, in the reign of Nebuchadnezzar himself, Jews. Babylon was a thoroughly mongrel city.

The United States, like Babylon, is a mongrel nation. The first settlers in America were English. By 1790, almost two hundred years later, ninety percent of the population was still English and Scots, with ten percent being from Germany,

Holland, Ireland, and France. The rising slave trade was responsible for bringing hundreds of thousands of the black race from Africa; famine brought many more from Ireland; the need for cheap labor to build the railroads brought the Chinese. Political and religious persecutions in Russia resulted in thousands more coming from the Ukraine. Jews came to escape persecution and for better business opportunities. The aftermath of World War Two saw many more come. By 1980, more than one million Cubans had migrated to escape communism; the Vietnam War caused an influx of millions of Vietnamese, Cambodians, and Laotians. And so they have come from all over the world — from India, Japan, Sweden, Poland, and all nations. And, like Babylon, after World War Two we brought in German scientists to help build our space program. Currently, the biggest influx is from Central America to escape from war in that area, and thousands cross our borders from Mexico. Quoting *The Immigration Time Bomb* by Palmer Stacy and Wayne Lutton:

> America is being invaded. Every day thousands of foreigners illegally enter our country. Over two million illegal aliens will come this year, most of them penetrating our porous two thousand-mile border with Mexico. Additional hundreds of thousands will arrive through our superficially inspected harbors and international airports. In 1975, General Leonard Chapman, commissioner of the Immigration and Naturalization Service, warned: "Illegal immigration is out of control." The total number of illegal aliens already in the United States may exceed twelve million — more than twice the size of the Soviet armed forces. President Ronald Reagan stated on October 19, 1983, that "this country has lost control of its own borders, and no country can sustain that kind of position."

The consensus of many, even President Clinton, is that within a few years, possibly by 2020, there will be no racial majority in the United States. Non-white populations are now giving more births to children than white populations. Hispanics alone are increasing in population statistics by more than one million a year, and this increase is to expand exponentially.

The majority land mass now known as the United States was first settled by white, Christian (mostly Puritan) people from Europe. Had this nation been settled by Moslems, it would be like Saudi Arabia; had it been settled by Buddhists, it would be like Southeast Asia; had it been settled by Hindus, it would be like India. We must wonder what the United States will be like when there is no racial or religious majority. Will God continue to shed His grace upon, and bless this nation, from sea to shining sea?

There are now so many languages spoken in our country it is almost like Babel after the confusion of tongues. Some states are considering laws to maintain education and communications in our common English language. Babylon used people from other nations to help build a mighty nation, but in the end the foreigners proved a detriment to survival. This is not to say Americans should not be proud of their heritage in being a refuge of safety for the oppressed and downtrodden, but on the other hand, we have indeed become much like ancient Babylon.

A few days ago an angry listener to our program called to berate me for giving European Protestants the credit for building this great nation. His argument was that our European ancestors had taken this land away from native Indians. Cluing in this callers' accent, I asked him where he was from. He responded that he was from Chile. I then asked him why he would come to such a racist country. He responded that he was fleeing an arrest and possible execution from a cruel Chilean dictator. Then I asked this gentleman if he was not pleased that we white, Protestant folks had founded a nation where he could find safety, liberty, and a good job.

Heaven forbid that anyone would ever call me a racist. I have traveled the world and eaten bread with every race and religion on earth. I could willingly live in a Beduoin tent and roam the deserts, or live in a bamboo hut in the Philippines. Like our native Oklahoman, Will Rogers, I have never met a person of a different color that I could not love. In Christ there is neither race nor color. Sin and rebellion is in the heart, not in the skin. Yet, we cannot take lightly God's absolute authority on this subject, "[God] hath made of one blood all nations of men for to dwell on all the face of the earth, and hath determined the times before appointed, and the bounds of their habitation."

Edward Tracy, in his book *The United States in Prophecy,* wrote:

> It was the solemn judgment of God that of one language and one people there should be many languages and many peoples. The motto of the United States is "E Pluribus Unum," which means "Out of many, one." Intentional or not, this is nothing less than effrontery, if you recall that lest the people of Babel should exalt themselves against God, He said, in effect, "Out of one, many." . . .
>
> Having a political structure, which is tantamount to a reversal of God's singular judgment against Babel, this country has certainly not been restrained from doing all that which they have been able to imagine — even so far as going to the moon.

Keeping in mind that Jeremiah 50 and 51 has a double application to old Babylon and the last Babylon, we read Jeremiah 50:12: "Your mother shall be sore confounded; she that bare you shall be ashamed: behold, the hindermost of the nations shall be a wilderness, a dry land, and a desert." The mother of the United States is England, and our nation did indeed confound England in the War of Independence. The reference to the "hindermost of the nations" does not mean the least of the nations, but rather the last of the nations, or a new nation. In Jeremiah's time, this could mean Babylon, except the land of the nation of Babylon has never become a wilderness and a desert. The land between the Tigris and Euphrates rivers is still one of the richest agricultural regions in the world; only the city declined and became mostly uninhabited over a time period of about six hundred years. In an end-time setting, the hindermost or newest of the great nations would, of course, be the United States.

Another verse in Jeremiah 50 gives another clue that Babylon could possibly be the United States: "How is the hammer of the whole earth cut asunder and broken! how is Babylon become a desolation among the nations!" (Jer. 50:23). A hammer is a carpenter's tool to drive nails. To hammer a person means to beat them down so they will submit to your will. In the way it is used in Jeremiah 50:23, it means to fashion or shape; in reference to a nation, its usage infers a powerful political force in the world. Since World War Two, the United States has been the hammer among nations, or at least the free world. At Potsdam, Franklin D. Roosevelt met with Josef Stalin to hammer out the shape of the post-war world. Eastern Europe was given to Russia, and the colonial empires of Europe, including England, were broken up. Winston Churchill was quoted as saying that he refused to be a partner in any political agreement that would bring about the dissolution of the British Empire. Nevertheless, the United States reshaped Europe through NATO, the Common Market, and the Marshall Foreign Aid Plan, which made West Germany a major industrial power. In the Orient, the United States helped to make Japan the most industrialized nation the world has ever seen. In Southeast Asia our hammer was dented, but we still have enough political prestige to affect the political shape of the Middle East. This is not to criticize our efforts to contain communism and help to shape a better world, but most of our foreign diplomatic attempts either backfire or come to nought. As it was at Babylon, so it still is today — it is God who rules in the affairs of men and nations and even sets over them the basest of men.

There are many parallels between the religious, commercial, and national Babylon of the last days and the United States. Only the unfolding of future events can verify this comparison. However, with the rise of Iraq to a military power of dimensions to cause a mobilization of many nations and threaten world peace, the emphasis of prophetic interpretation shifted back for a few years to the site of the once mighty world empire ruled by Nebuchadnezzar. Now it shifts again back to the United States. Where the pendulum will finally stop still remains a mystery.

Chapter 17
Iraq — Prelude to Armageddon

On March 29, 1971, an AP news release from Beirut, Lebanon, reported: "Iraq says it plans to rebuild the ancient city of Babylon, whose hanging gardens were among the seven wonders of the world. The project will cost about $30 million."

We determined to travel to Iraq and see for ourselves this ancient city of Nebuchadnezzar that was rising from the dust of history. So, on March 13, 1978, after a breakfast of Iraqi bread and fig preserves, served with thick, black, bitter coffee, the one hundred and three members of a tour group that I was leading boarded buses and headed out of Baghdad for Babylon on the Euphrates. We traveled westward at sixty-five miles an hour over a four-lane highway, passing kilns along the way that were turning out bricks for the reconstruction project.

Archaeologists had already excavated much of the ruins. The Germans had even removed the upper portion of the Ishtar Gate and reassembled it in a museum in Berlin. But large sections of the city were still recognizable, and it appeared that from five to ten percent of the buildings were in the process of being restored. While in Iraq, we went south to see the city of Ur, the home of Abraham. We also went north to Nineveh and saw the remains of this once mighty metropolis.

Just before our arrival in Iraq, Israel launched a military campaign into Lebanon to clean out PLO terrorist groups, so the entire Middle East was on war footing. We were supposed to have taken sleeper cars to Nineveh, but the Iraqi government was using these facilities to move troops by train through Turkey and Syria into Lebanon. So our group was given two coach cars, hooked on to an ammunition and troop train. We were told to stay put in our seats and not move. I still remember the Iraqi military police walking up and down the aisles, all night long, beating their palms with huge baseball bat-like clubs. We needed little additional incentive to keep us very still and quiet.

Saddam Hussein's (Black) Golden Image

Nebuchadnezzar was informed by Daniel that he was the head of gold on the image the king saw in his dream (Dan. 2). But, the head of gold was to give way to three succeeding kingdoms. This displeased the king, so he subsequently made an entire image of gold. This was Nebuchadnezzar's way of showing Daniel's God that his kingdom would last forever; and his city, Babylon, would be an eternal city.

History confirms that in 538 B.C. Daniel's prophecy regarding the fall of Babylon to the Medo-Persian Empire came to pass. But the monetary factor that figures in the rebuilding of Babylon today is not yellow gold, but black gold — oil. Oil, according to the explanation given by many geologists, is the decayed residue of plant and animal life. The one place in all the world that has more oil than any other is the small country of Kuwait, the site of the biblical Garden of Eden. This means that where Kuwait is today, there must at one time have been a veritable jungle. From this vast oil pool center, lesser pools spread out into southern Iraq, southern Iran, and northeast Saudi Arabia. Within an area roughly encompassing a circle two hundred miles in diameter, with the center in

Kuwait, lies over fifty percent of the world's oil reserves.

When we traveled through Iraq in 1978, army camps were much in evidence. Soldiers were everywhere, and from the highways we could see armored columns training for combat. Most of the armaments at that time came from Russia. Iraq is an area roughly the size of California, with a population of seventeen million — seventy-five percent Arab; fifteen percent Kurd; ten percent Turk and others. The size of the nation's army in 1978 was one million. During the Nixon and Ford administrations, the U.S. State Department became concerned about Iraq's growing militarism and close alliance with Russia. Agents from the CIA convinced the Kurds, who had a natural hostility toward the Arabs anyway, to begin guerilla activities in the north with pledged U.S. support. But then Henry Kissinger negotiated a favorable oil deal with Baghdad. No support came from the U.S. and the poor Kurds were offered like sacrificial lambs — rebel leaders were hanged and thousands of others were shot. These are the same Kurds that Saddam Hussein killed with nerve gas and mustard gas during the war with Iran. Much of the problem this nation is now facing in the Middle East is of our own making.

In 1978, as we traveled to southern Iraq, the closer we came to Ur, the more evident oil fields became. But what did the main items of interest that we saw in Iraq (oil fields, rebuilding of Babylon, and advancing militarism) have in common?

The perpetuation of a Babylonian (Babel) kingdom with an eternal city as the pearl of Chaldean pride has never died in the minds and hearts of the descendants of the royal family of ancient Babylon. The seating of Saddam Hussein as the sole dictator of Iraq in 1979 revived the image of Nebuchadnezzar. In fact, Saddam Hussein claims to be a reincarnation of Nebuchadnezzar, and on the bricks used to rebuild Babylon, the names of both (Nebuchadnezzar and Saddam Hussein) appear side by side in the baked clay.

It may be debated as to whether the motivation for the building of a relatively small nation into a military superpower was for aggression or for the pursuit of the dream of Nebuchadnezzar to control the world, and to be worshipped by all nations as a god. But if the gaining of territory and power was the only objective, why spend hundreds of millions of dollars (the first thirty million dollars was only a drop in the bucket) to rebuild an ancient city with evidently no commercial or military importance.

The most valuable commodity in the world to mankind is, of course, fresh water. The second most important is food. The third most valuable item to the contemporary social and economic structure is energy — energy to provide heating, cooling, lighting, machine power, automobile and airplane transportation. Oil is the best source of energy. Of the industrial powers, Japan and Europe import practically one hundred percent of their oil, and the United States imports over sixty percent of the oil needed. If the world would pay thirty dollars a barrel for oil as it did in the oil crisis of the 1970s (which it is doing in 2000), then it would just as readily pay one hundred dollars a barrel if forced to do so. Saddam Hussein reasoned that the man who could control the world's oil market could become the most powerful man on earth, and over fifty percent of the world's oil was at his doorstep.

Presidents Johnson, Nixon, and Ford had built the army of the Shah of Iran into the third most powerful military force in the world. But President Carter had practically abolished the CIA and the revolution that overthrew the Shah caught him by surprise. He was too indecisive to react. Then followed the humiliating capture and imprisonment of Americans as hostages. The United States was hailed as the Great Satan by Khomeini and the Ayatollah became the most despised man by the free world.

Saddam Hussein of Iraq then seized this opportunity to add the oil fields of Iran to his kingdom on the road to glory. Although Saddam Hussein reasoned that Iran would be an easy pushover, he did not reckon with an army that had been trained and equipped by the United States. For eight long years, as long as World War One and World War Two combined, Iran and Iraq fought to a standstill. The main difference between the two antagonists was that Iraq had more outside support. Saddam Hussein had unlimited credit to buy weapons on the world market, and the battlefield became a training ground for his army. President Reagan and the U.S. State Department even explained away as an accident a missile attack by Iraq on a Navy vessel in which American lives were lost. Also overlooked, conveniently, was the unmerciful killing of innocent civilians, including the Kurds in Iraq, with poison gas. Saddam Hussein literally got away with murder. Although the war with Iran ended in a stalemate, Saddam emerged as the winner in the eyes of the world. While he did not get much oil, he did salvage a few pieces of Iran's territory.

One nation that was never deceived by Saddam Hussein's long-range plans for rebuilding the Babylonian Empire was Israel. In 1981 Israel made an air strike against a nuclear plant in Iraq to prevent the development of atomic and hydrogen bombs. Had Israel not destroyed this nuclear facility, Iraq might today have nuclear weapons, which would make the present situation far more dangerous. That the Iraqi dictator is still trying to make nuclear weapons is quite clear from the attempt to funnel atomic bomb parts to Baghdad through Russia and Pakistan. Another attempt was made by Saddam Hussein to import parts for a huge howitzer that would propel a projectile capable of delivering nerve gas or an atomic warhead distances of up to five thousand miles. The man responsible was an ordinance expert whose plans for such an enormous gun had been rejected by the U.S. Army. He evidently sold the idea to Hussein, but then the inventor himself was assassinated in Brussels in March 1990. When in Israel in June 1990, I inquired as to whether Mossad operators or CIA agents had terminated the man, but I was told the killing was probably done by Iraqi agents when the deal began to go sour.

Although Saddam Hussein has not been able to obtain super terror weapons, other than poison gas, he evidently felt there was no one who would dare challenge his move to take over Kuwait. Only an unprecedented quick response by President George Bush kept the Iraqi army from continuing on south and capturing the Saudi oil fields. Saddam Hussein in 1990 controlled thirty-two percent of the world's oil reserves; had he gotten the oil fields of Saudi Arabia, he would have controlled over fifty percent, and possibly become the most powerful man on earth. He could have created havoc in the industrialized world.

Other Interested Participants

The United Nations Security Council, realizing the danger presented by Saddam Hussein to the most valuable energy source on earth, quickly voted embargo sanctions against Iraq. The Arab League failed to suggest any acceptable solution, but some offered token forces to join the Americans in Saudi Arabia.

Kuwait was a British-established national entity founded in 1961 to protect foreign oil interest in what could have been the original Garden of Eden, because as noted, it is here that is located more underground oil reserves per acre than any other comparable area in the world. Kuwait in 1990 had a population of approximately two million. Its size is only sixty miles from border to border, comprising an area of sixty-nine hundred square miles. The ruling class in this constitutional monarchy is exceedingly rich. Most native Kuwaiti families import civil workers and personal servants from other countries. Most Arab and/or Moslem countries were jealous of Kuwait and some, like Jordan, actually supported Saddam Hussein in his attempt to capture this oil prize on his march to restoring Babylon to its former glory. Only the fear that they might be next kept other Arab nations from entering the war on the side of Iraq. Had Saddam been more careful to make this overt aggression more of a religious cause, he might have gotten away with it.

A Reuter news release reported on August 12, 1990:

> A statement issued by the group [The World Islamic League] after an appeal by Saddam Hussein to Arabs and Moslems to save the Holy Places of Mecca and Medina from foreign forces said, "We wish Iraqi president Saddam Hussein would call on Arabs and Moslems to liberate al-Aqsa Mosque from Jewish hands."

In order to help defray or retard Middle East participation on the side of Iraq, President George Bush forgave Egypt an eight billion dollar foreign debt, gave Lebanon to Assad of Syria, promised Jordan additional millions in foreign aid, and there were doubtless U.S. goodies for other interested parties.

Saddam Hussein repeatedly attempted to draw Israel into his war by sending SCUD missiles against Tel Aviv. While this tactic was partially successful, it did not result in other active Arab military intervention.

As high noon and the showdown between George Bush and Saddam Hussein approached toward the latter days of 1990, the United States could count thirty-eight other participating allies. True, some sent only a banner, flag, or water truck. The U.S. provided eighty percent of the frontline fighting force, along with airplanes, ordinance, and quartermaster units. Approximately fifteen percent of the desert army was sent by England, France, Germany, and a few other European allies, and five percent or less was contributed by other nations. President Bush indicated this united attempt to avert and punish aggression by an army made up of many was a prelude to the New World Order which he envisioned. In January 1990, Dr. Robert Lindsted and I had attended the National Religious Broadcasters Convention at the Sheraton Hotel in Washington, D.C. Eight times in his speech before the convention, President Bush referred to the New World Order. Each time the president mentioned the New World Order, the forty-five hundred delegates would jump to their feet and applaud. As far as I could tell, Dr. Lindsted and I were the only ones who remained seated. We stared at each other in amazement. What kind of New World Order was President Bush referring to — the government of Antichrist mentioned in Revelation 13, or the government that Jesus Christ would established when He returned? Inasmuch as President Bush did not mention the Name of Jesus Christ in his address, we had to suppose that he was talking about a future international governmental arrangement by man, which would in due course become centralized under one head.

In November 1990 as military forces began to build up in Saudi Arabia, predictions of a serious nature came from the Pentagon about how terrible the coming war would be when the assault to evict Saddam Hussein's army from Kuwait began. The United States Armed Forces put in a requisition for fifty thousand body bags. The name chosen for the Kuwaiti operation was Desert Storm. I had led tours to four continents, many of a missionary nature. Therefore, I seized upon this opportunity to lead a tour to the Middle East and call it Desert Shield. This tour would land in Israel and include a prayer session for peace in the Middle East and God's protection for our soldiers in Saudi Arabia. This sunrise prayer session would be on top of Mount Hezekiah. Why Israel named this mountain after King Hezekiah is not known, as there is no indication that the king ever visited this mountain. Mt. Hezekiah is the highest mountain in the Southern Negev Mountain Range. The peak is just thirty feet from the Egyptian border, and from this summit in Israel we can look across the Gulf of Aqaba due east and see Jordan, and to the southeast see Saudi Arabia. It was the perfect place for a united prayer service to God by Christians from many different churches to intercede for His solution to the Middle East crisis and protection for American armed forces. I had alerted Israeli governmental dignitaries, who said they would come, and I envisioned at least one thousand Christians from the United States gathering in a Desert Shield sunrise prayer vigil.

But not so fast! Even though I have led some thirty-five tours to the Middle East, and on some had several buses, not many Christians wanted to test their faith by being caught in what could have been a major conflict. Nevertheless, thirty-three members of our Desert Shield did meet on top of Mt. Hezekiah, with Israeli representatives, and convened for an hour-long prayer service. The remark we often heard during our Desert Shield mission in Israel was, "You people must either have a lot of faith, or you are terribly dumb."

During the remainder of 1990 and January 1991 the build-up of armies from many nations continued to pour into Saudi Arabia. Dire predictions poured in from the media about what a terrible and costly war in terms of human life this conflict would be. It was thought that perhaps at the last minute Saddam Hussein would back down and leave Kuwait, but it did not happen. Finally, on February 24, 1991, the war began. The united allied army, which was eighty percent American, attacked. We have read about the miraculous Six-Day War that Israel waged against four Arab armies; this was a three-day war.

Needless to say, the massive military buildup by the Desert Storm participants, and especially the United States, amounted to monumental overkill. In just seventy-two hours the Iraqi military forces lost 260,000 soldiers — 175,000 were captured and 85,000 were killed (*2000 World Almanac*, pg. 809). The U.S. forces lost 296, and approximately half of these were killed in combat accidents. One of the biggest problems in the war's aftermath was what to do with 49,704 leftover body bags.

Now who can say that our November 1990 Prayer Shield vigil on top of Mt. Hezekiah was in vain? We are instructed quite plainly in Scripture that the prayers of righteous men avail much. Daniel's prayers got God's attention on behalf of the prophet's nation, Israel. Perhaps God did honor the prayers of thirty-three U.S. citizens offered on top of Mt. Hezekiah on a cool and windy morning in November of 1990 on behalf of our soldiers. Who knows but that our prayers were at least partly responsible for the 49,704 empty body bags.

In vengeance, the Iraqis set fire to the Kuwaiti oil fields as they retreated back to Iraq. The huge clouds of black smoke that blotted out the sun, spreading across the Persian Gulf and over Iran, seemed to be almost a fulfilling of Isaiah 34:8–9: "For it is the day of the LORD's vengeance, and the year of recompenses for the controversy of Zion. And the streams thereof shall be turned into pitch, and the dust thereof into brimstone, and the land thereof shall become burning pitch."

Perhaps the burning oil fields of Kuwait were a forewarning of what all the oil fields of the Middle East will become when the Antichrist initiates the three and one-half years of desolation following his act of abomination of the Temple Mount.

That the military machine of Saddam Hussein suffered a seeming catastrophic defeat was evident. However, the allied New World Army of President Bush and the United Nations did not pursue the retreating Iraqis. The majority of the Iraqi military forces escaped. The possible reason there was no pursuit and complete annihilation was that the United States and the Europeans understood that in spite of Saddam Hussein's aggression and ambitions, he was still considered a family member of the Moslem and Arab worlds. Ill will could have been garnered that in the future would create more problems for the oil-hungry West than destroying Saddam's army would gain. It was also reasoned by President Bush that after suffering such a seemingly fatal defeat, that Hussein himself would be totally disgraced and deposed by a new Iraqi government. This did not happen, because the Arab and Moslem nations have always manifested a resilience in bounding back from defeat to emerge even stronger. This Arab mindset and determination is evidenced in the reported statements of Arab leaders: **We can lose ninety-nine wars against Israel — all we have to do is win the one hundredth war.**

The sanctions, inspections, embargoes, and armament restrictions placed on Iraq by the United Nations from 1991 to 2000 are well known, so there is no need to bore the reader with these agonizing details.

The conclusion is that in spite of all his defeats and economic problems and restrictions, Saddam Hussein continues to maintain one of the largest and most powerful armies in the world. According to the International Institute for Strategic Studies, Iraq maintains an army of 1,037,500 (active or reserve), supported by twenty-seven hundred tanks, over three hundred first-line aircraft, adequate artillery and missile compliments. Iraq's armed forces are judged to be stronger than those of Ukraine, France, Germany, Italy, Syria, Great Britain, Spain, Israel, and Mexico (*2000 World Almanac,* pg. 215). This in itself merits continued attention and concern. However, this was not a troubling consideration for Dr. Logsdon in 1968.

Having the will and determination, it is possible in this age for the weak with a few weapons of nuclear destruction, to become as strong as the strongest (Joel 3:10,11). Although seemingly not reasonable, it is still possible for Iraq in conspiracy with China, Russia, Iran, Pakistan, Syria, Egypt, or Libya, to be the Babylon of Revelation that will be destroyed in one hour.

Chapter 18

Destruction of Babylon in Isaiah

Bible prophecy in some respects is like watching a ninety-minute movie which covers a fifty-year timespan. A time segment of ten, twenty, or thirty years may be omitted from the movie because what happened during that time is not essential to the main story. For example, in Isaiah 61 the prophet sees Christ at His first coming to die for sin, and then goes immediately to His second coming as the King of Glory.

Over one hundred years before Babylon destroyed Jerusalem, Isaiah had warned King Hezekiah of Judah that this nation would do exactly what it would do (2 Kings 20). The prophet also revealed a prophecy concerning the eventual destruction of Babylon. This prophecy is set forth in detail in Isaiah 13. It is evident that God gave Isaiah this revelation, not only as a warning to Judah, but also a sign of the end of the age to those living in the last days.

> The burden of Babylon, which Isaiah the son of Amoz did see. Lift ye up a banner upon the high mountain, exalt the voice unto them, shake the hand, that they may go into the

gates of the nobles. I have commanded my sanctified ones, I have also called my mighty ones for mine anger, even them that rejoice in my highness.

— Isaiah 13:1–3

According to Daniel, God rules in the affairs of men and nations. Also Daniel revealed that God commands angelic messengers to deal with rulers and the princes of this world. Isaiah states first in this chapter that this was not just a message from God by Word, he actually saw this judgment to come against Babylon. Isaiah 13 is a revelation, just as the Apocalypse is a revelation. An army banner is a signal for the troops to assemble, and this banner mentioned by Isaiah is to be a high mountain, a challenge to many nations.

Isaiah in the vision sees God in His anger against Babylon, and angelic messengers going to the nobles of many nations to assemble them to battle. This is not the battle of Armageddon, because even nations that praise the Lord are to assemble. It is interesting to note that Israel was not involved in the Desert Storm war against Iraq in 1991, while traditional Christian nations like England and the United States were involved.

The noise of a multitude in the mountains, like as of a great people; a tumultuous noise of the kingdoms of nations gathered together: the LORD of hosts mustereth the host of the battle. They come from a far country, from the end of heaven, even the LORD, and the weapons of his indignation, to destroy the whole land.

— Isaiah 13:4–5

In the Desert Storm war against Iraq, the soldiers from the United States with all their tanks, artillery, and missiles indeed were from a far country, and as indicated in this prophecy, other nations from afar off sent military personnel and battle gear. Even in World War Two not this many armies from so many nations, thirty-nine in all, had been assembled on one battlefield. Isaiah also noted judgment would come from heaven, and Iraq was pounded by bombardments from planes and cruise missiles days before the ground battle began. Isaiah also indicated this would be a noisy army, even attacking with a deafening roar. On television, planes were shown taking off to bomb Iraq with their afterburners roaring, and then in the battle the tanks, missiles, and artillery booming away, there was never a tumultuous noise like this even when the Medes and Persians were assaulting Babylon. As noted, in 538 B.C. even some citizens of the city did not know there had been a change in government. Isaiah could not have been referring to the fall of Babylon in 538 B.C., because Media and Persia were only two nations and both were next door neighbors. The prophet saw in the vision many nations coming from the end of the earth against Babylon. This prophecy, I believe, was fulfilled in the Desert Storm war of 1991.

We note also that Isaiah said these nations had come "to destroy the whole land," but he **did not say they would destroy the whole land**. With the Iraqi army in a disorderly retreat, the Desert Storm army could have destroyed the whole land, but President Bush ordered a cease fire and a sudden halt to the advance. This was something that was difficult to understand at the time, but his orders did fulfill Isaiah's prophecy. "Howl ye; for the day of the LORD is at hand; it shall come as a destruction from the Almighty. . . . Behold, the day of the LORD cometh . . ." (Isa. 13:6,9).

It is to be noted that Isaiah did not report that this assault upon Babylon by many nations from the end of the earth was in the Day of the Lord, the Tribulation period. He said this battle would be a sign that the Day of the Lord would be near. Verses seven through eighteen describe in some detail judgments that will occur in the Tribulation, judgments mentioned also by other prophets, Jesus Christ, and Apostle John. "And Babylon, the glory of kingdoms, the beauty of the Chaldees' excellency, shall be as when God overthrew Sodom and Gomorrah" (Isa. 13:19).

The prophet now takes us into the Tribulation. This is an incident different from the one mentioned in the first half of the chapter. Babylon, neither the city nor the country, has to this date been destroyed like Sodom and Gomorrah. If this judgment in verse nineteen does not apply to the restored city of Babylon, or the nation of Iraq, could it apply to the United States as Dr. Logsdon concludes? To be, or not to be, that is the question.

The prophet also had a further word to say about Babylon: "Go ye forth of Babylon, flee ye from the Chaldeans, with a voice of singing declare ye, tell this, utter it even to the end of the earth; say ye, The LORD hath redeemed his servant Jacob" (Isa. 48:20).

The Jews taken to Babylon did not have to later flee from the Babylonians. When they did return, Babylon had fallen to Medo-Persia, and the Persians willingly welcomed the return, even providing the needed funds and logistics for rebuilding the Temple and Jerusalem. So, could this prophecy refer to a future flight of five million Jews, the present U.S. Jewish population, from America? Very possible.

Chapter 19

Jeremiah Against Babylon

God revealed to Isaiah the rise and fall of Babylon one hundred years before Nebuchadnezzar destroyed Jerusalem and the Temple. However, the prophet Jeremiah lived in Judah during the time of the Babylonian invasion, and predicted by inspiration of the Holy Spirit the length of time that the Jews would be in captivity to Babylon:

> And this whole land shall be a desolation, and an astonishment; and these nations shall serve the king of Babylon seventy years. And it shall come to pass, when seventy years are accomplished, that I will punish the king of Babylon, and that nation, saith the LORD, for their iniquity, and the land of the Chaldeans, and will make it perpetual desolations.
>
> — Jeremiah 25:11–12

We know by history and Daniel 9:1–2 that the captivity of Judah by Babylon did last for seventy years, but the second part of the prophecy relating to the perpetual desolation of Babylon has not been fulfilled to this day. A more detailed and progressive prophetic view of Babylonian history from the time of Neb-

uchadnezzar to the second coming of Jesus Christ was set forth
by the prophet in Jeremiah 50 and 51.

> The word that the LORD spake against Babylon and against
> the land of the Chaldeans by Jeremiah the prophet. Declare
> ye among the nations, and publish, and set up a standard;
> publish, and conceal not: say, Babylon is taken, Bel is con-
> founded, Merodach is broken in pieces; her idols are con-
> founded, her images are broken in pieces. For out of the north
> there cometh up a nation against her, which shall make her
> land desolate, and none shall dwell therein: they shall re-
> move, they shall depart, both man and beast. In those days,
> and in that time, saith the LORD, the children of Israel shall
> come, they and the children of Judah together, going and
> weeping: they shall go, and seek the LORD their God. They
> shall ask the way to Zion with their faces thitherward, say-
> ing, Come, and let us join ourselves to the LORD in a perpet-
> ual covenant that shall not be forgotten.
>
> — Jeremiah 50:1–5

It is evident from the beginning of Jeremiah's prophecy against
Babylon that he was not speaking primarily about the Babylon of his day. The prophet understood that he was speaking
of the distant future — "in those days, and in that time." Jeremiah understood that after seventy years a remnant would
return from Babylon, but beyond that return, he must have
understood about another return from all the world when the
children of Israel and the children of Judah would both come
weeping to the land seeking the Lord their God (Messiah) to
make an everlasting covenant that would never be forgotten.
This did not occur when the Jews came back from Babylon in
the third and fourth centuries B.C. It will be in "those days"
and in "that time," that the great desolation of Babylon, including the entire land of Chaldea, will take place. God has

never forgiven the descendants of Esau for their crimes against Israel, and on a national basis, God has not forgiven Babylon.

> Remove out of the midst of Babylon, and go forth out of the land of the Chaldeans, and be as the he goats before the flocks. For, lo, I will raise and cause to come up against Babylon an assembly of great nations from the north country: and they shall set themselves in array against her; from thence she shall be taken: their arrows shall be as of a mighty expert man; none shall return in vain.
>
> — Jeremiah 50:8–9

In these verses another warning is given to aliens in the land to get out before judgment falls. The signal for the eventual desolation of the entire land of Babylon is the assembling of the armies of great nations. The weaponry of these armies are arrows shot, or launched, by experts, indicating high technology. As a result of the arrows, it is not stretching the meaning of the scriptures to infer they will bring about the sudden desolation of Babylon as occurred at Sodom and Gomorrah. Have arrows shot from bows ever brought about the desolation of any nation? What kind of arrows must these be?

On page one of the August 18, 1990, *Jerusalem Post,* under the heading "Arrow Missile Tested," we read the following:

> At 3:35 p.m. the Arrow Missile [was] shot into the sky at slightly under ten times the speed of sound. . . . The test proves the Arrow can be launched and can reach operational speed. . . . The U.S. Strategic Air Command is running the project on the American side, while Israel Aircraft Industries is building it here.

Israel has approximately one hundred atomic bombs and a dozen hydrogen bombs, according to common news media reports. It seems more than coincidental that Israel's latest missile program is called Arrow.

> Your mother shall be sore confounded; she that bare you shall be ashamed: behold, the hindermost of the nations shall be a wilderness, a dry land, and a desert. Because of the wrath of the LORD it shall not be inhabited, but it shall be wholly desolate: every one that goeth by Babylon shall be astonished, and hiss at all her plagues. Put yourselves in array against Babylon round about: all ye that bend the bow, shoot at her, spare no arrows: for she hath sinned against the LORD.
>
> — Jeremiah 50:12–14

If Babylon is the United States, then the mother would be England. However, in light of the rise of Iraq and the rebuilding of the city of Babylon, the mother could refer to the Arab race and the Islamic religion. The Moslem leaders of Saudi Arabia, the homeland and foundation of Islam, have openly stated that they are ashamed of the Iraqis in that they have denied the faith and murdered their own brothers. As in other prophecies referring to the final destruction of Babylon, we see again in the preceding verses warnings about the coming desolation of that nation and the shooting of arrows by many nations to produce the extreme devastation. In verse twelve it should be noted that the prophet expresses surprise that the "hindermost" of nations would attract such opposition from the assembly of nations. According to *Webster's Dictionary*, hindermost means the lowest part, or the most posterior part, like the tail. Hindermost, if referring to the United States, could mean the last of the great nations to rise, or if referring to Iraq, could mean a seemingly small and lowly nation.

And indeed, the world is amazed that a nation the size of California, with one-fifteenth the population of the United States, could suddenly endanger the major energy source of the world and command a worldwide mobilization. Jeremiah wonders that this lowest of nations would challenge an assembly of great nations, but this is exactly what occurred in the Middle East crisis of 1990. This little nation, with only seventeen million people, challenged the will of the General Assembly of the United Nations.

> Cut off the sower from Babylon, and him that handleth the sickle in the time of harvest: for fear of the oppressing sword they shall turn every one to his people, and they shall flee every one to his own land.
>
> — Jeremiah 50:16

At the time that Iraq invaded Kuwait, there were millions of workers, businessmen, and technicians from other nations in that little country. The oil-rich economy established a super-wealthy native and foreign elite who employed workers and household servants from the poor nations. In Iraq, millions from other countries had found work in the oil fields as well as the third largest military establishment in the world. While Iraq imports large quantities of certain types of food, the fertile land between the Tigris and Euphrates rivers produces most of the nation's vegetables. Because of the long war with Iran and the manpower shortage, farm workers came from Egypt, India, Pakistan, and other countries — two million from Egypt alone. With the invasion of Kuwait, these workers dropped their hammers, saws, brooms, plows, and hoes, and fled westward to Jordan where they piled up on the desert border by the hundreds of thousands.

In the next few verses, the prophetic scene merges the immediate future with the distant future, and then changes again to the very end of the age:

> And I will bring Israel again to his habitation, and he shall feed on Carmel and Bashan, and his soul shall be satisfied

upon mount Ephraim and Gilead. In those days, and in that time, saith the LORD, the iniquity of Israel shall be sought for, and there shall be none; and the sins of Judah, and they shall not be found: for I will pardon them whom I reserve.

— Jeremiah 50:19–20

Carmel, Bashan, and Mount Ephraim are a part of Israel today, as well as the northwest area of Gilead to the east of the lower part of Galilee. Bashan has not been occupied by Israel since the days of King Solomon, that is, until after the 1967 war. Bashan is today known as the Golan Heights. While these areas are occupied by Israelites today, the iniquity of Israel and the sins of Judah have not been pardoned, nor will they be until all Israel cries out to Jesus Christ, ". . . Blessed is he that cometh in the name of the Lord" (Matt. 23:39). As mentioned by Jeremiah, it will be a part of Israel whom God will reserve to be pardoned from sin and enter into an everlasting covenant with God (Zech. 13:8–9).

A sword is upon their horses, and upon their chariots, and upon all the mingled people that are in the midst of her; and they shall become as women: a sword is upon her treasures; and they shall be robbed. . . . As God overthrew Sodom and Gomorrah and the neighbour cities thereof, saith the LORD; so shall no man abide there, neither shall any son of man dwell therein. Behold, a people shall come from the north, and a great nation, and many kings shall be raised up from the coasts of the earth. They shall hold the bow and the lance: they are cruel, and will not shew mercy: their voice shall roar like the sea, and they shall ride upon horses, every one put in array, like a man to the battle, against thee, O daughter of Babylon.

— Jeremiah 50:37, 40–42

The prophets often explained warfare in the last days in the common language and technology of their day. If they had named, or accurately described, tanks, airplanes, and other weapons of contemporary use, the Bible would have been discarded as the work of madmen. The prophet does say that the sounds of this great army would be like the roar of the sea — tanks driven by seven hundred horsepower and planes roaring through the sky. In these verses Jeremiah again refers to the mingled people who would be in Babylon at the time of judgment, and like Isaiah, Jeremiah compares the coming destruction of Babylon to that of Sodom and Gomorrah.

Next Jeremiah sees the king of Babylon as the armies of many nations gather against him:

> The king of Babylon hath heard the report of them, and his hands waxed feeble: anguish took hold of him, and pangs as of a woman in travail. Behold, he shall come up like a lion from the swelling of Jordan unto the habitation of the strong: but I will make them suddenly run away from her: and who is a chosen man, that I may appoint over her? for who is like me? and who will appoint me the time? and who is that shepherd that will stand before me? . . . At the noise of the taking of Babylon the earth is moved, and the cry is heard among the nations.
>
> — Jeremiah 50:43–44, 46

Nebuchadnezzar built up the city-state of Babylon into a world empire. He emerged from an obscure beginning to become the most powerful man in the world. He was a cruel, proud, and egotistical man. He burned victims who refused to worship him as a god. Saddam Hussein also rose from an obscure background. He got his start in politics as a revolutionary against the government of Iraq. He escaped execution by fleeing to Egypt, where he continued his education. After his political friends gained power in Iraq, Saddam returned and quickly rose in political stature. As Iraq's chief security officer, he hanged nine Jews on the streets of Baghdad in 1969. Although he wielded much power in the socialist government of Iraq, and was instrumental in promoting the rebuilding of Babylon, he was not made the absolute dictator. He quickly identified those he could not trust in his own party, and it is reported that he personally shot everyone that was singled out. Saddam, on one occasion, shot a top general for daring to suggest an alternative military action. There is little doubt, according to CIA intelligence reports, that if President Bush would not have taken immediate action, the Iraqi dictator would have invaded Saudi Arabia and possibly become even greater than Nebuchadnezzar.

But in prophesying about the king of Babylon that would be destroyed like Sodom and Gomorrah, Jeremiah did not say Nebuchadnezzar, but rather "the king of Babylon." Saddam Hussein has indeed come up like a lion, like the swelling of the Jordan at flood stage. He has gained the attention and fear of the world, but Jeremiah prophesied that when the chips were down, the king of Babylon would become as weak and helpless as a woman in childbirth. While Jeremiah's prophecy about the king of Babylon could refer to Belshazzar at the taking of old Babylon by the Medes and Persians, the prophecy more aptly applies to Saddam Hussein, or the Antichrist, ruler of the last Babylon.

The concluding prophecy against Babylon in Jeremiah 50 foretells that when the assembly of nations finally attack and destroy it, even the earth will shake and the cry of the people will be heard within the nations. The earth moving seems to indicate tremendous atomic explosions, and with modern television, the cry of the people could be heard in the nations of the world.

Thus saith the LORD; Behold, I will raise up against Babylon, and against them that dwell in the midst of them that rise up against me, a destroying wind; And will send unto Babylon fanners, that shall fan her, and shall empty her land: for in the day of trouble they shall be against her round about. . . . Flee out of the midst of Babylon, and deliver every man his soul: be not cut off in her iniquity; for this is the time of the LORD's vengeance; he will render unto her a recompence.

— Jeremiah 51:1–2, 6

The most feared weapon Saddam Hussein had in 1990 was poison gas, mainly mustard gas and nerve gas. There was also the threat of biological warfare. Hussein had used both weapons against dissident racial groups in his own country. When SCUD missiles were dropping from the skies on Israel, every Israeli was issued a gas mask. In the United States, there remains much concern about Iraq using terrorists to bring in containers of death-dealing microbes and release them on the side of a major city where the wind will carry the deadly germs or viruses across. In a metropolitan area like New York, Chicago, or Los Angeles, millions would die. It has been reported that federal medical teams are training hospitals in one hundred twenty of our largest cities how to deal with such a crisis. In World War Two, Germany used poison gas, but sometimes the wind would change and blow it back across German lines. The "destroying wind" that Jeremiah indicated would bring judgment against Babylon could have had a prophetic reference to Desert Storm, but this reference could also apply to a more deadly destruction during the Tribulation. We also might wonder if this prophecy has a connection to Revelation 7:1–3:

And after these things I saw four angels standing on the four corners of the earth, holding the four winds of the earth, that the wind should not blow on the earth, nor on the sea, nor on any tree. And I saw another angel ascending from the east, having the seal of the living God: and he cried with a loud voice to the four angels, to whom it was given to hurt the earth and the sea, Saying, Hurt not the earth, neither the sea, nor the trees, till we have sealed the servants of our God in their foreheads.

Nebuchadnezzar the king of Babylon hath devoured me, he hath crushed me, he hath made me an empty vessel, he hath swallowed me up like a dragon, he hath filled his belly with my delicates, he hath cast me out. The violence done to me and to my flesh be upon Babylon, shall the inhabitant of Zion say; and my blood upon the inhabitants of Chaldea, shall Jerusalem say. Therefore thus saith the LORD; Behold, I will plead thy cause, and take vengeance for thee; and I will dry up her sea, and make her springs dry.

— Jeremiah 51:34–36

It may appear cruel and unjust for such a terrible judgment to be pronounced upon any nation, especially by a loving and merciful God. But God is not only merciful, not willing that any should perish, He is also a just God. Babylon has never as yet paid for the rape, plunder, and destruction of Jerusalem and the Temple some twenty-five hundred years ago. We know that the Word of God declares that whosoever defiles the Temple, him will God destroy. And so God has said to Israel through Jeremiah the prophet, do not concern yourself with vengeance upon Babylon, I will take care of it in my own way and time. "And thou shalt say, Thus shall Babylon sink, and shall not rise from the evil that I will bring upon her: and they shall be weary. Thus far are the words of Jeremiah" (Jer. 51:64).

Chapter 20
John Against Babylon

Besides end-time judgments pronounced against Babylon in Isaiah, Jeremiah, and the Book of Revelation, others are scattered throughout the Bible. For example, we read in Ezekiel 32:11–15:

> For thus saith the Lord God; The sword of the king of Babylon shall come upon thee. By the swords of the mighty will I cause thy multitude to fall, the terrible of the nations, all of them: and they shall spoil the pomp of Egypt, and all the multitude thereof shall be destroyed. I will destroy also all the beasts thereof from beside the great waters; neither shall the foot of man trouble them any more, nor the hoofs of beasts trouble them. Then will I make their waters deep, and cause their rivers to run like oil, saith the Lord God. When I shall make the land of Egypt desolate, and the country shall be destitute of that whereof it was full, when I shall smite all them that dwell therein, then shall they know that I am the Lord.

In the extremity of the age, two old enemies, Egypt and Babylon, faced each other across the border between Arabia and

Iraq. It seems apparent from the prophecy of Ezekiel that even though Babylon will be desolated like Sodom and Gomorrah, the king of Babylon will be involved in the desolation of Egypt. As a result of this judgment that will come upon both nations, their rivers will run like oil. Remarkable! In the event of war, millions of barrels of oil could run into the Tigris and Euphrates rivers, fulfilling this prophecy. An expressed concern of many nations who depend upon Middle East oil is the purposed or accidental rupture of the oil fields in Iraq, Kuwait, Iran, and Saudi Arabia. This partially happened in February 1991.

More details about the coming desolation of Egypt are given in Ezekiel 29:8–12:

> Therefore thus saith the Lord GOD; Behold, I will bring a sword upon thee, and cut off man and beast out of thee. And the land of Egypt shall be desolate and waste; and they shall know that I am the LORD: because he hath said, The river is mine, and I have made it. Behold, therefore I am against thee, and against thy rivers, and I will make the land of Egypt utterly waste and desolate, from the tower of Syene even unto the border of Ethiopia. No foot of man shall pass through it, nor foot of beast shall pass through it, neither shall it be inhabited forty years. And I will make the land of Egypt desolate in the midst of the countries that are desolate, and her cities among the cities that are laid waste shall be desolate forty years: and I will scatter the Egyptians among the nations, and will disperse them through the countries.

Not only will Babylon be desolated like Sodom and Gomorrah, but many of the cities of Egypt will be made desolate in the same manner. Also, Egypt will be in the middle of many other cities and nations in the Middle East that will be made desolate so that for forty years even a dog will not be able to pass through and live. This prophecy was given to Ezekiel over twenty-five hundred years ago, yet there is no more accurate description of what will happen if an atomic war occurs in that part of the world. In other prophecies relating to the judgment of nations in the day of the Lord we are informed that Damascus (Syria) will be a ruinous heap; the mountains of Lebanon will be on fire; Arabia will be scorched with terrible heat, etc. According to Daniel and Jesus Christ, the time of great desolation will occur when the Antichrist breaks his treaty with Israel and commits the Abomination of Desolation.

The fiery destruction of Babylon is the apex of Great Tribulation judgments, because it is the religion of Babylon that has deceived the world through a multitude of deceptions. Even while the ancient city of Babylon lay underneath the sands of the Euphrates, religious Babylon, also called Mystery Babylon, permeated the world under a multitude of occultic worships. In these last days, the New Age movement with its many-faceted forms of mysterious worships in crystals, astrology, incantations, meditations, gods of illuminations and ascended masters, is an assortment of Babylonian mysteries.

Martin Luther, after going to Rome and witnessing the corruption, opulence, and blasphemy of the Vatican, proclaimed that the Catholic Church was Mystery Babylon and Pope Leo was the Antichrist. Many Protestant theologians and ministers have agreed with Luther, and today when traveling in predominantly Roman Catholic countries and visiting cathedrals like Notre Dame in Paris, St. Peters in Rome, and the Cathedral of Toledo near Madrid, we are tempted to join with others in making a similar comparison between the Vatican and the great whore of Revelation 17. The wealth on display in these cathedrals and monasteries (jewels, silver, robes, and idols of solid gold statues weighing up to a thousand pounds) in the midst of extreme poverty sickens our very soul. Hislop, in *The Two Babylons,* makes a good case for the Catholic Church carrying on the Babylonian priesthood, and as previously noted, the symbol of Nimrod, the obelisk, stands in front of St. Peter's Cathedral in Rome, and in front of Sophia Haggia in Istanbul (Constantinople).

Let us assume that Roman Catholicism is the Mystery Babylon of Revelation, and the pope is the false prophet. How would this theoretic possibility fit into the religious scenario of the Tribulation? In light of what we know today, with the United Nations finally reaching its envisioned potential, what if the U.N. were to appoint a central religious agency to coincide with the international political authority? This, as viewed from a one-world perspective, would certainly be desirable. Religious fanaticism in the Moslem world, Orthodox Judaism, Hinduism, Buddhism, and apostate Christendom would need to be polarized and directed toward a single humanistic goal — peace on earth!

Would all the different religions, sects, and cults have to concede, adhere to, or profess a unity of doctrine or liturgy? Not at all. The only common expectation would be to agree to pursue a goal of world peace under the leadership of a single authority. The most recognized single religious personality in all the world who would project the image of world peace for the good of all mankind would, without controversy, be the pope. Mystery Babylon, the culmination of the religion of Nimrod, is not envisioned by John to be a single entity, but the "mother of harlots," the incorporation of many harlots into one family. While we do not profess to know every turn in the course of coming events, and neither do we say that the Roman Catholic Church will be the shelter for the church of the false prophet, in light of current world developments, we are beginning to understand how it could happen. All major world religions, including the New Age movement, are waiting for their own particular messiah. It would be a readily acceptable announcement to declare one personality as a god of all who will take his mark and follow him to a world order of peace and prosperity. Mystery Babylon fulfills the plan of Nimrod to bring all races, languages, and nations back into a common world where all divisions of mankind are unified into the worship of one political head (Rev. 13).

The enforcement of the mark of the beast upon humanity and the worship of the Antichrist as god concludes the need for a religious order. God puts into the mind of the beast a plan to destroy Mystery Babylon (Rev. 17:17). The annihilation of the world congress of religions, with all offices, priests, monks, ministers, etc., must take place soon after the Antichrist sits in the Temple of God, showing himself to all the world as God.

National Babylon is not to be confused with Mystery Babylon, even though there may be a religious identification common to both. While the judgment of the great whore seems to be foretold to occur at the beginning of the second half of the Great Tribulation, the destruction of national Babylon is somewhat more difficult to place. From the Old Testament it appears certain that Babylon is to be destroyed and made desolate in the great and terrible day of the Lord — the Tribulation period — within seven years of the second coming of Jesus Christ. That the destruction and judgment of Babylon is to occur before the battle of Armageddon appears obvious because Babylon is not listed among those nations whose armies will be decimated with the brightness of His coming. And while John seems to indicate the destruction of national Babylon near the end of the Great Tribulation, in Revelation 14:8 he indicates the same judgment to occur in the first half.

Many have erred in basing prophetic chronology on current events that appear to have pregnant eschatological promises. But from what we overtly see taking place in the Middle East, and the respective role of the superpowers in that developing conflict, we can understand how a sudden and massive desolation of Iraq could trigger an invasion by Russia down through Turkey and over the Golan Heights into Israel.

An increasing percentage of the world's wealth goes to the nations of the Persian Gulf for oil. How long it will take, or exactly what events must transpire, to fulfill the conditions and situations set forth in describing the judgment of Babylon like Sodom and Gomorrah cannot be fully determined at this time. But for the first time, we who are comparing the signs of the times with the prophetic Word may be reasonably assured that the long shadows of the coming great and terrible day of the Lord are being cast upon the desert sands of Saudi Arabia, Iraq, Iran, Syria, Jordan, and Egypt. This we know for certain, the apostle John saw the coming destruction of Babylon as taking place in one hour on a particular day. God knows the day the destruction of Babylon is to take place, and in 1 Thessalonians 5:1–5, Paul admonished that Christians should not let the day of the Lord come as a thief in the night.

Christians today have many reasons to expect the coming of the Lord at any time. Therefore, ". . . let us, who are of the day, be sober, putting on the breastplate of faith and love; and for an helmet, the hope of salvation" (1 Thess. 5:8).

Chapter 21
The World Beyond Babylon

On a cold March morning, sixty-two–year–old Gerald Vincent Bull was shot to death by assassins as he left his apartment building in Brussels. Such assassinations are common to the world of the 1990s, but there was something very unusual about this one. Bull had the proven record of being a ballistic and ordinance genius who had performed valuable service to the United States, Canada, and Israel. But at the time of his death in Brussels, the artillery genius was working for Saddam Hussein to develop a supergun called "Project Babylon."

In World War One the Germans developed three enormous howitzers with a range of seventy-four miles. These guns were used to lob shells into Paris, but they disappeared after the war. Even in World War Two the largest artillery guns had a range of only twenty-five miles. However, in 1973 Gerald Vincent Bull sold Israel fifty thousand shells that would bombard Damascus from the Golan Heights, but these were never used. Evidently, Israel still has them in storage. Bull was also reported in *Fame* magazine to have helped Israel neutralize electronic equipment at the raid on Entebbe.

In 1965, the daughter of the German who designed the Paris Gun (also called Big Bertha) provided Bull with the blueprints of the World War One artillery monster. Subsequently, Bull went to Barbados, where he could operate in relative secrecy, and came up with a one hundred ten foot gun that would propel a two hundred pound shell a distance of twenty-five hundred miles. Another model was developed that would propel a twelve hundred pound projectile a distance of six hundred miles. The United States and Canada turned down Bull's offer to incorporate such weapons into their armed forces, favoring instead already developed rockets.

Bitterly disappointed, Bull found a ready customer in Saddam Hussein. According to the *Jerusalem Post* of September 15, 1990, Bull designed a 155-howitzer that was made in Austria, far superior to anything the United States has. Three hundred of these artillery weapons went to Iraq. Bull was also financed by Saddam Hussein to develop three long-range multipurpose guns that would hit targets anywhere in the Middle East, including Jerusalem. These guns would fire conventional explosives, poison gas, or nuclear warheads. Contracts were let in seven European nations and the parts were then sent to Iraq to be assembled. But the clandestine plot began to break down simply because it was too diversified. While forty-four parts of the first long-range howitzer did reach Baghdad, the remaining eight essential parts were intercepted. Bull was assassinated by either CIA, Mossad, or Iraqi agents.

Only our imagination can contemplate what horror Saddam Hussein could have created had he been able to complete the assembling of these huge, long-range guns. It seems likely, from the interception of nuclear bomb pieces in London bound for Iraq, that atomic shells were contemplated. A prototype of one of the guns, called "Baby Babylon," was test-fired at Mosul, just across the Tigris River at the site of the old city of Nineveh. Of what use this artillery weapon may be to Iraq in the future is unknown.

Besides the NATO nations of Europe, the United States,

Russia, China, and Israel, at least a dozen third world nations have the ability to develop and deliver mass destruction weapons. Saddam Hussein is just an example of what could happen in almost any nation where a strong man takes control of the government with ambitions to become a world dictator.

The United Nations was established as a viable international organization in June 1945 in San Francisco. The U.N. was actually a rebirth of the old League of Nations, and for all intents and purposes, other than being a forum for international griping and complaints, the organization has been no more effective than its former model. It has, however, provided large salaries and plush homes for international loafers, mostly at the expense of American taxpayers.

The United Nations was founded as "an international organization dedicated to the maintenance of international peace and security, and composed of nations subscribing to the principles and obligations enumerated in the Charter of the United Nations" (*Funk and Wagnall Encyclopedia*). As stated in the charter, member nations were to settle their differences through peaceful negotiations within the office of the U.N. rather than resorting to war or force of arms. During the time the U.N. has been in existence, there have been no world wars of the scope of World War One and World War Two. However, there have been a multitude of lesser wars and revolutions: the Korean War, the Vietnam War, the Afghanistan War, Cuba, Angola, Nicaragua, Lebanon, three wars between Israel and the Arab Alliance, China, Cambodia, Bosnia, Kosovo, etc. Perhaps the main reason for no extensive international war has been the fear of nuclear annihilation, not U.N. influence.

However, when Saddam Hussein threatened the world's major oil supply, with a resulting threat of financial shockwaves that could have overturned the international banking system, the United Nations finally acted in unison to condemn the aggression and endorsed United States' plans to stand up against the bully of Baghdad. Some of the nations like Egypt and Syria supported the U.S. position, along with some military units, simply because they hate anyone in the Arab world standing taller than they stand. Russia gave lip service to the U.N. effort, but at the same time oppose military action and keeps several thousand technicians and military advisors in Iraq to ensure that the United States did not use military action. But the one issue that finally brought the U.N. to a unified position was not to save the peace, but rather, to save the oil.

On September 11, 1990, the president of the United States, George Bush, appeared on television before the entire world and made the following announcement:

> A new partnership of nations has emerged. . . . Out of these troubled times, a New World Order can emerge. . . . A hundred generations have searched for this elusive path to peace, while a thousand wars raged across the span of human endeavor. Today that new world is struggling to be born . . . a world where the rule of law supplants the rule of the jungle; a world in which nations recognize the shared responsibility for freedom and justice; a world where the strong respect the rights of the weak. . . . This is the vision I shared with President Gorbachev in Helsinki.

Almost two thousand years ago, another man stood on Mount Olivet in Jerusalem, and looking forward in time to the very end of the age, He said:

> . . . Take heed that no man deceive you. For many shall come in my name, saying, I am Christ; and shall deceive many. And ye shall hear of wars and rumours of wars: see that ye be not troubled: for all these things must come to pass, but the end is not yet. For nation shall rise against nation, and

kingdom against kingdom: and there shall be famines, and pestilences, and earthquakes, in divers places. All these are the beginning of sorrows.

— Matthew 24:4–8

Even so-called conservative voices like the *National Review* have been caught up in the fantasy of the New World Order:

New international order . . . that the post-Cold War should, as far as possible, be one of peace and stability. This is not global altruism. As a world power with economic presence in all continents, the U.S. has strong interests in the international order that trade and overseas investment require.

Patrick Buchanan, in an editorial that appeared in the *Daily Oklahoman* of September 15, 1990, said of the above statement that appeared in *National Review:* "Excuse me, this is not conservatism; it is Trilateralism, the foreign policy of David Rockefeller. . . ."

The Council on Foreign Relations, the Trilateral Commission, the Club of Rome, the European Union, international communism, the United Nations, international bankers, the World Council of Churches, the Roman Catholic Church, the New Age movement, and dozens of other pseudo-political and religious organizations and groups we could name, were all hailing the facade of world peace through world government in the wake of the U.N. action against Iraq. But each group or organization sees in a New World Order an opportunity to attain to its own economic, political, or religious goal.

From the prophetic Word of God we can know:

- National Babylon will be destroyed in a fiery judgment.
- Israel will be forced to sign a peace treaty that will concern the land.

- Russia will invade Israel over the Golan Heights.
- There will be a world political order.
- There will be a world religious order.
- The world religious order will be destroyed by the world political order.
- The leader of the world political order will break the treaty with Israel.
- The armies from out of all nations will move against Israel.
- The international army will be destroyed by Jesus Christ at His coming.
- Jesus Christ will then take the government of all the world upon Himself.
- There will be peace and prosperity in all the world for one thousand years.

There are many other events foretold in the Bible that will occur within the seven-year period preceding the return of Jesus Christ, and except for the last three items listed, we cannot say for sure in which order the others will occur.

We are in no way predicting the Rapture of the church and the beginning of the Tribulation in the immediate future. There has been far too much date-setting for the Lord's return in recent years. However, there are strong and striking parallels in the developing situation in the Middle East today with events God declares must come to pass before Jesus Christ returns.

President George Bush said at his meeting with Mikhail Gorbachev in Finland: "If the nations of the world, acting together, continue as they have been, we will set in place the cornerstone of an international order more peaceful than any that we have known."

We agree with President Bush that it is time to lay the cornerstone of a new international order. But the cornerstone that will be laid is not the United Nations cornerstone, but Jesus Christ Himself, the Stone that will strike the image of all Gentile power and authority at the Battle of Armageddon (Dan. 2).

. . . Behold, I lay in Sion a chief corner stone, elect, precious: and he that believeth on him shall not be confounded. Unto you therefore which believe he is precious: but unto them which be disobedient, the stone which the builders disallowed, the same is made the head of the corner, And a stone of stumbling, and a rock of offence. . . .

— 1 Peter 2:6–8

Chapter 22

U.S.A. in Isaiah?

It is to be noted that a question mark is purposely placed after the heading of this chapter, because it is a matter of interpretation — and we might add, loose interpretation — that the United States is referenced in the prophecies of Isaiah. The reference most in question is chapter eighteen. "Woe to the land shadowing with wings, which is beyond the rivers of Ethiopia" (Isa. 18:1).

Even the first word that introduces this chapter is a matter of controversy. Dake says of "woe" as used here, "Woe, not Ho, as some would say. The word is used here of a judgment." Faussett says, ". . . not woe, but ho, call attention." Eerdman says, "The prophecy commences with *hoi,* which never signifies *heus,* but always *voe* (woe). Here, however, it differs from ch. xvii." Eerdman continues to express the opinion that "woe" as used in Isaiah 18 means "compassion rather than anger." When Jesus used this word in reference to Chorazin, Bethsaida, and Capernaum, it was in a judgmental sense. However, in checking a dozen or more references by scholars, so-called or otherwise, "woe" in Isaiah 18:1 could mean anything from, "I'm going to blow you off the map" to "Have a nice day." Therefore, the meaning of "woe" (*hoi*), depends on the context in which it is used.

The nation of Ethiopia as mentioned in Isaiah 18 involves much more territory than the area of present-day Ethiopia. The word for "Ethiopia" in the Hebrew text is *Cush*. Cush in Isaiah's time involved present-day Ethiopia, Somalia, Sudan, and two-thirds of Egypt.

The judgment-of-nations section of Isaiah concerns the known world of that day from an Israeli perspective: Babylon, Syria, Assyria, Moab, Damascus, Egypt, Cush, etc. Bible commentaries, footnotes, encyclopedias, dictionaries, etc., simply copy each other in explaining that the nation identified in Isaiah 18 can only be Ethiopia. Having gone out on this limb, then the history and geography of Ethiopia, from Isaiah's time backward, must fit. Therefore, the expositors must indulge in all kinds of theological and historical contortions, the majority of which is ninety-nine percent conjecture or imagination. If Isaiah had known the name of the country, people, or nation referenced in chapter eighteen, he would have named it just as surely as he named Babylon, Syria, and Assyria. Isaiah clearly indicated that although he did not know the name of this nation, it was beyond the rivers of Cush — by rivers doubtless meaning the Blue Nile, White Nile, and Upper Nile as it flows through present-day Egypt. Isaiah was prophesying about a nation, then or in the future, west of the Nile River. This nation would have to be located in West Africa, North America, or South America. If it was in Europe, then or in the future, he would have said beyond the Great Sea. The reason that most scholars, so-called or otherwise, do not even consider that Isaiah was prophesying about a future nation is that they do not want to acknowledge that the prophetic Word has a meaning for Christians today.

In attempting to describe this nation so that future generations, even you and I, could possibly have an idea just who this country was, Isaiah said it was a "land shadowing with wings." How do the "scholars" identify a shadowing of wings with Ethiopia? Dake said this is a reference to the dreaded TSETSE fly. TSETSE FLY? Ha!

There are seven Hebrew words for "shadow" so translated in the King James Version. Some refer merely to shade, or the shadows of people or objects. In other scriptures the Hebrew word for "shadow," *tsalmaveth*, is associated with darkness or death. In no place in the Bible do I find any of the seven Hebrew words for "shadow" refer to the shadow of a tsetse fly, sitting, flying, or otherwise. The Hebrew word for "shadowing," *tselatsal*, is found only in Isaiah 18:1, and it could well be interpreted as "overshadowed," as the glory of God overshadowed the Holy of Holies, or as Jesus would have overshadowed Jerusalem with His protection (as a hen gathers her chicken), but they would not.

The emblem of the United States is the eagle, and today we are certainly a nation shadowing with airplane wings, perhaps more than any other nation. Our office is in the flight pattern of planes landing at the Oklahoma City Will Rogers World Airport. At almost any time during the day, I can look out my window and see planes flying over our office. I certainly do not say that "shadowing with wings" has to apply to the United States, but it could. Tsetse fly? Nah!

Another clue to the identity of this nation seems to be that it sends ambassadors over the seas to other continents. Churches and Christian organizations have certainly sent missionaries to almost every country in the world, and mission stations today are maintained in the majority of nations. I am a member of the Gideons organization, and the Gideons send representatives to eighty percent of the nations in the world. The nation's Peace Corps organization sends American men and women by the thousands to third world nations. American businessmen also travel to practically every nation. Also, all three branches of the national government send ambassadors to other countries. Every time I turn on CNN, I see one of our government representative getting off an airplane in some other country. The United States has sent millions abroad to fight and oppose evil tyrants — the Spanish-American War, the Philippines, China, Mexico, World War One, World War Two, Korea, Vietnam, Haiti, Somalia, the Middle East, Bosnia, Kosovo, etc. I served three years in the South Pacific in World War Two. It is certainly true that U.S. involvement in some of these conflicts has been morally questionable and ill-advised, but in the majority, like World War Two, they have been of a defensive nature or for a good and just cause.

In any event, I cannot think of any nation in the history of the world who has sent more representatives or ambassadors, whether good or bad, abroad over the globe than the United States.

Another clue so thoughtfully provided by Isaiah is that this nation west of the Nile that sends ambassadors around the world, is also a people terrible from their beginning. There are nine different Hebrew words translated "terrible," or variable forms of "terrible," in the King James Bible. The Hebrew word for "terrible" in Isaiah 18:2 is *yare*, which means, as stated in *Young's Concordance,* "To be feared, reverenced," or we could say, to be respected. The United States was founded by immigrants fleeing from religious and political persecution. They came to America willing to fight for what they considered to be God-given rights. They fought the Indians, the French, and then the British, and in wars already noted. Today, the United States is generally acknowledged as being the strongest nation in the world militarily. And, until the present Clinton administration, the United States has been respected by other nations as the moral leader of the world. Certainly, this clue could well point to the United States as the unknown nation of Isaiah 18. Isaiah adds the word "hitherto" (He. *he-leah*), which means "beyond," "yonder," or "future," "not yet, but will be." This means that this nation probably was not in existence when the Lord gave Isaiah this prophecy.

Yet another clue to this unknown nation's identity is that it will be a nation that is "scattered and peeled." In meaning, these two words cannot be separated. There are many different Hebrew words translated "scatter" or "scattered," but one only Hebrew word for "peeled." The Hebrew word translated "scattered" in Isaiah 18:2 is *mashak,* which does not mean to scatter like paper, sticks, or even people. It means "to prolong," "draw out," or "over time." The Hebrew word for "peeled" is *marak,* which means to polish, like a gem, more than peel, like fruit. Within the context, this means the people comprising this nation would be unfinished, rough, discounted at the beginning, but over a period of time the real purpose and full potential of this country would come to fruition. While this description could apply to other nations in West Africa, North America, and South America, I can think of no other nations on these continents that it could apply to more than the United States.

Continuing in our search to find and name this nation beyond the rivers of Cush, Isaiah noted yet another identifying factor. He wrote that this nation would be "meted out and trodden down." Again, there are several Hebrew words, with different meanings, interpreted "mete" and "meted" in the King James Version. The Hebrew word for "mete" in Isaiah 18:2 is *qav,* which means to "line," "rule," "mark off" (not measure like a bushel of wheat). In Europe, Asia, and Africa, nations have histories of thousands of years, but the history of the United States, even considering colonial times, is less than four hundred years. In England, for example, sheep, cattle, and animal trails became lanes and roads for the knights to travel from one castle to the next castle or from one village to the next village. Later, homes and businesses were built along these trails and lanes and they became roads. Of course, in modern times nations like Germany have straightened many of their road and highway systems, but many of the roads that were at one time cattle trails still exist. The same pattern of establishing roads was the practice of Americans in colonial days, but being a new nation, this practice was corrected in time. I refer to an explanation of this clue in Isaiah's prophecy from *America in Prophecy* by Dr. E. F. Webber:

"A nation out and trodden down." Or as it could be interpreted, "A land measured under foot." We learn from early history that at about the time Florida and Ohio were taken into the United States, a law was passed making it mandatory that all public land be surveyed by the North Star and divided into square mile sections, then subdivided into quarter sections, a half mile square, the size of a homestead. We were the first country ever to survey and divide the land according to the ranges with the North Star, and all our land from the western edge of Pennsylvania to the Pacific Ocean, and from Canada to Mexico, has been surveyed by lines of measurements, then staked out in quarter sections after this law of General Surveys had been passed. Now, the prophet wrote about this twenty-seven hundred years ago, more than a thousand years before America was discovered by Columbus. The prophet told about the fact that our land would be surveyed into sections whose lines point due north and south, east and west.

A descriptive phrase, "meted out and trodden down," may not require further explanation or interpretation. However, leaving no clue uninvestigated in our search for this nation's possible identity, we look at the two words, "trodden down." The Hebrew word translated in the King James Version for "trodden down," is *mebusah,* which means "treading down." In that the land mass now comprising the continental area of the

United States was uncultivated and untouched as European immigrants settled the New England states and then spread across the continent to the Pacific Ocean, laying out roads, cultivating the land, and establishing towns, it could be said that our land was indeed meted out and trodden down. Another meaning of "trodden down" or "treading down" is taking possession of, or conquering. We read in Daniel 7:23 about the fourth beast described in this chapter, the Roman Empire (which also extends to the revived Roman Empire). This beast, we read, "shall devour the whole earth and tread it down." As explained in Daniel 2, the Roman Empire broke into many smaller empires: British Empire, German Empire, French Empire, Spanish Empire, etc. These empires annexed colonies, lands on every continent — all of Australia, all of North America, all of South America, all of Africa, all of Europe, Asia and the islands of the sea. All of the United States was owned by the French Empire, the British Empire, and the Spanish Empire.

The last clue afforded by Isaiah as to the identity of this mystery nation is that it is a nation "whose land the rivers have spoiled." There are at least a dozen different Hebrew words that are translated "spoil," "spoiled," or other different noun, verb, or gerund variations. *Spoil* in the sense of captured booty is a noun. Of course, parents can *spoil* (verb) their children by giving them more than they need. The Hebrew word for "spoiled" In Isaiah 18:2 is *baza,* which means "to take as a prize or a treasure." The annual flooding of the Nile was indeed of great benefit to Cush and Egypt. It is true that rivers are a great blessing to any nation, but especially is this true of the many rivers across the United States. Isaiah was not saying that the rivers of this nation would damage or ruin the land, but rather that these rivers would be of great value to the land. While this clue could apply to many nations, I think it has a special meaning to our own country.

That this nation described by Isaiah would be a great nation in the world at the end of the age seems to be stressed by the prophet in that he goes directly from verse two into the Kingdom Age in verses three through six. In the Kingdom Age, when the Lord Jesus Christ reigns over the nations with a rod of iron from Jerusalem, the leaders of all nations must go up to Jerusalem from year to year to worship Him. If the leader of a nation does not go up to worship the Lord in Jerusalem and learn of His laws, then that nation will be judged. If representatives from Egypt refuse to worship the Lord in Jerusalem, then no rain will fall on that nation (Zech 14:17).

Isaiah concludes his prophecy about this mystery nation: "In that time shall the present be brought unto the LORD of hosts of a people scattered and peeled, and from a people terrible from their beginning hitherto; a nation meted out and trodden underfoot, whose land the rivers have spoiled, to the place of the name of the LORD of hosts, the mount Zion" (Isa. 18:7).

I almost did not include this chapter on Isaiah 18 in the book. I have previously rejected the possibility that this prophecy could even remotely refer to the United States, because I had read so many explanations to the contrary. Admittedly, this prophecy by Isaiah about this unidentified country may not refer to the United States, but I at least believe it could. If the United States is the mystery Babylon that will be destroyed in one day, in one hour, then there is no connection. Perhaps whether Isaiah 18 references our nation depends upon the citizens of the United States right now. Jesus said that if Israel would accept Him as the Messiah, then John the Baptist would be Elijah; but if Israel did not receive Him, then Elijah would truly come later. Perhaps we are in similar conditional judgment.

This should encourage and inspire Christians in the United States to pray and work even more fervently for a revival in our churches and a repentance for sin in our land. Then, in the Millennium, a future president and attorney general could be going to Jerusalem to worship Jesus Christ in person and learn of His laws.

Chapter 23
Other Prophetic Possibilities

The referencing of the United States within the prophetic scenario has been alluded to by many Bible scholars. One such reference to consider is Ezekiel 38:13:

> Sheba, and Dedan, and the merchants of Tarshish, with all the young lions thereof, shall say unto thee, Art thou come to take a spoil? hast thou gathered thy company to take a prey? to carry away silver and gold, to take away cattle and goods, to take a great spoil?

Chapters thirty-eight and thirty-nine of Ezekiel relate prophetically to a great power to the north of Israel, identified as Gog. The setting for an invasion of Israel by Gog, along with named allies, is when Israelites have been gathered back into the land from many nations. It is obvious that this is a Tribulation, or near-Tribulation, prophecy. The consensus of theologians who study the prophetic Word is that Gog is Russia. As explained in the verse above from Ezekiel 38, some nations will protest, including the young lions of Tarshish. Some have suggested that inasmuch as the national emblem of the British Empire is a lion, that the young lions refer to either colonies of the British Empire, or former colonies that have gained independence, like Australia, Canada, and the United States.

Perhaps a more credible reference would be Daniel 7:4: "The first was like a lion, and had eagle's wings: I beheld till the wings thereof were plucked, and it was lifted up from the earth, and made stand upon the feet as a man, and a man's heart was given to it."

This prophetic vision given to Daniel concerns four beasts: a lion, a bear, a leopard, and a terrible and awesome beast. Empires are represented by carnivorous beasts. Nations become empires by preying upon and eating up other nations. The fourth beast, which had ten horns, plainly represented the kingdom of Antichrist which Jesus Christ will destroy when He returns to set up His kingdom (Rev. 19). All four beasts come up out of the Great Sea. The Great Sea usually, if not always, refers to the Mediterranean Sea.

The interpretative controversy relating to the four beasts is to place the beast in a Time of the Gentiles historical, progressive setting, or to place all four beast in the last generation at the end of the age. The historical interpretation identifies the lion as Babylon; the bear as Medo-Persia; the leopard as Greece; the fourth beast Rome, and the ten horns as the revived Roman Empire, the empire of Antichrist.

A secondary interpretation places all four beasts in an end-time setting:

Lion. The lion is an emblem of the British Empire. The British Empire did control the Mediterranean Sea and occupied Palestine and Egypt after World War One. The eagle is the emblem of the United States. The eagle wings (U.S.) were plucked off the lion. After World War Two, England lost its colonies and is no longer an empire — no longer a beast. England and the United States did have complete control of the Mediterranean Sea until 1960. The United States continues to have much involvement in Israel and the entire Middle East.

Bear. In the late 1950s and 1960s, Russia began to arm Egypt, Jordan, Syria, and Iraq. Russia also enlarged its fleet in the Mediterranean Sea, and armed Syria, Egypt, and Iraq. After Russia's allies lost two costly wars against Israel (1967,1973), Russian influence waned, but might be revived as indicated in Ezekiel 38. The emblem of Russia is a bear.

Leopard. This beast has four wings of a fowl and its power and authority is delegated. While the United States continues to arm Egypt, Israel, and Jordan, the main outside military presence is maintained by the United Nations. This beast may represent the present military and political conditions in the Middle East today.

The Terrible Beast with Ten Horns. That the revived Roman Empire is the European Union is the consensus of the vast majority of pre-millennial advocates. That the E.U. today is becoming stronger and getting more involved in Middle Eastern affairs is evident.

Although the United States is not specifically identified by name, as noted previously, it is included in the nations with which God has a controversy; and if still in existence, this nation will be judged by Jesus Christ when He rules all nations with a rod of iron.

Chapter 24

Mystery Babylon Checklist

God called and separated Israel for a particular purpose. Israel was given a vision as to their divine destiny. To attain the fulfillment of God's plan and purpose for the nation, outlines and laws were given to chart their progress toward this goal. As long as Israel remained on their destined course God protected the nation and blessed it above all other nations. Through the prophets of God Israel was warned continually not to forget "the Lord your God."

Of those whom God's calls and blesses, God expects much — total obedience. When Israel forsook God's laws, worshipped idols, and forgot its mission, they were punished more than any other nation. No nation in history has suffered more than the descendants of Abraham, Isaac, and Jacob.

It is my conclusion after considering all evidences, that God called the United States for a particular purpose, a special mission. With the chunks of the Roman Empire still vying for world supremacy and embroiled in both political and religious oppression (even England), a new nation came into being to offer mankind a new hope. The founders of this nation gave it just laws based on God's ordinances for human government. This new nation gave immigrants fleeing from oppression the liberty to come to the knowledge that there is a God who created all things, and that there is a mediator between God and man — Jesus Christ (1 Tim. 2:1–6). In being obedient to these laws and faithful to the vision that God gave the nation, the United States has been blessed above all other nations, even more than Israel was blessed under the judges and kings.

The United States has been faithful to allow the unrestrained preaching of the Gospel of Jesus Christ. This nation has sent missionaries abroad to other nations, races, and languages to feed the hungry, heal the sick, and save souls from hell by saving faith in Jesus Christ. The United States has been a home for Jewish refugees, and even in the year 2000 there were more Jews in America than in Israel. The United States has fought in two World Wars to save the world from cruel dictatorships, and hundreds of thousands of our citizens have suffered and died in these wars. The United States has served as a model for human government to other peoples seeking justice and liberty.

Above all these reasons for God blessing the United States is that this nation has helped to sustain a Jewish nation, and it is probably to this end that this country has become the strongest in the world, while the Soviet Union imploded from within.

There are doubtless many other reasons God has called and blessed the United States in becoming a leader of nations in these last days. However, the United States today is not the nation it was even forty years ago. The following is a checklist as to where the United States has changed:

1. Taking God Out of Education

And even as they did not like to retain God in their knowledge, God gave them over to a reprobate mind. . . .

— Romans 1:28

The first step in the decline and fall of a nation is taking God out of education. Without wisdom from God, men become only smart fools (Rom. 1:22). In the *New England Primer,* the book out of which the children of the delegates to the Constitutional Convention were taught, students were taught the ABCs from the Bible. Example:

> C — Come unto Christ all ye that labor and are heavy laden and He will give you rest.
>
> E — Except a man be born again, he cannot see the kingdom of God.

From the *New England Primer* students had to know the answers to the following questions before they could pass to another grade:

> Who is the Redeemer of God's elect?
> How did Christ being the Son of God become man?
> What offices doth Christ execute as our Redeemer?
> How doth Christ execute the office of a prophet?
> How doth Christ execute the office of a priest?
> How doth Christ execute the office of a king?

If a student today in the public school system were to just read out of the *New England Primer* in class, he could be expelled. If a teacher in the public school system were to teach out of the *New England Primer,* he could be fined, fired, or jailed, or be subject to all three.

2. Sexual Immorality and Perversion

> For this cause God gave them up unto vile affections: for even their women did change the natural use into that which is against nature: And likewise also the men. . . .
>
> — Romans 1:26–27

When God and the Bible are taken out of education, the boys and girls are left with no moral guidelines, and pornography, abortions, pervasive fornication, illegitimate children, divorce, and broken homes follow. According to actual statistics, the number of children born out of wedlock has increased six hundred percent since 1950. Abortions per one thousand women of child-bearing age range from 2.7 in Wyoming to 44.6 in Nevada. The average for the fifty states is approximately 15.0 per one thousand women — **but in Washington, D.C.,** our nation's capital, the percentage is 154.5, **ten times the national average**. Of graduating high school seniors, 49.1 percent have used drugs and 81.4 percent use alcohol.

"[Fools have] changed the glory of the uncorruptible God into an image made like to corruptible man, and to birds, and fourfooted beasts, and creeping things" (Rom. 1:23). Using a mindless theory of evolution, agnostics, atheists, humanists, and anti-God proponents have captured the school systems and corrupted it while most Christians have joined the "five foolish virgin" club and sleep on.

3. Vile Affections
The Scriptures speak of natural affections and vile affections. It is natural for men to love women and women to love men. God calls the reverse "vile affections." It is natural for a bird to care for its young, or even a vicious beast like a female alligator to watch over its eggs. A mother cannot help but to love her baby, because this is a natural affection. Without natural affection, there would be no life. Sexual perversion is not only unnatural, it is vile. But what is even worse is when a nation not only condones it, but encourages it:

> Who knowing the judgment of God, that they which commit such things are worthy of death, not only do the same, but have pleasure in them that do them.
>
> — Romans 1:32

Homosexuality is applauded on television, in the movies, and even in government. President Clinton is too busy to speak to the National Religious Broadcasters annual convention, but he is never too busy to speak at the annual Gay-Pride Convention. He often boasts about having two thousand homosexuals in his administration. Several states either have, or are considering, recognizing homosexual partners as a legal marriage. According to a Reuters news release dated June 9, 2000, Ford, General Motors, and Chrysler have joined ninety other major U.S. companies in granting marital status to their one-half million homosexual employees. God has warned that this will destroy any nation.

4. "It's The Economy, Stupid"

James Carville, President Clinton's political mover, coined this phrase when the Clinton administration came under criticism. The psychological projection that the citizenry is supposed to embrace is that even though President Clinton had sex in the White House with a woman other than his wife, or that he has become a worldwide example of the cleverest liar, it's okay as long as the economy is good.

It appears tragic that while Serbian Christians were trying to hold on to a territory that has always belonged to them, against Moslems from Albania, the United States launched a vicious war against them. The Serbs held down twenty Nazi divisions in World War Two. Hitler may have won the war if he could have thrown these divisions against Russia. Hundreds of thousands of Serbs have died fighting the Moslems when these hordes from Turkey and the Middle East tried to conquer Europe. If it had not been for the Serbs, there may not have been a United States.

And while the United States has been a friend to Israel, Carter, Bush, and Clinton have attempted to trade the land God gave to this nation to others for pieces of worthless paper.

This land is God's land, and no president has a right to give it away.

Christians can be killed and enslaved in Sudan, yet our government is silent.

The same week Congress, with President Clinton's blessing, approved the establishing of normal trade relations with China, we received the following letter from one of our contacts in the underground church:

You asked about recent information concerning our mutual friend. I don't know what you read in the paper, but I can tell you that over the past month there have been many troubles in the Guangdong Province. Since last September, Li has been arrested fourteen times, two of which were for fifteen days. His last arrest was for fifteen days and he was treated badly during this time. Yes, he was chained up the entire time. What they did was they shackled his ankles two times. Then they put a bar in-between the shackles that spread his feet apart wider than his shoulders. He had to wear these the entire fifteen days. For the first three days they also cuffed his hands and fastened them to his feet. There was a ring in the center of the bar between his ankles and they fastened his hands there. He was bowed over in this position for three full days. He thanked God that after they finally released his hands he did not have any damage to his spine. With his feet still in shackles they forced him to labor from six a.m. to eleven p.m. every day. He had to make Christmas lights to be sold to America. He had to make four thousand to five thousand per day or he would be whipped with a belt. He saw others who received this treatment and they were whipped till they bled. With God's help he was able to make his quota. When he was released on a Tuesday, he was warned that if he went to the village again and preached, they would come after him. The same day more than ten officers went to the village meeting and they warned the Christians there also. On the following Tuesday the authorities showed up in force, but so did the people, more than five hundred came to the first meeting. The authorities brought loudspeakers and blasted the people with rock music trying to disrupt the meeting. Quietly, they read from the scriptures, sang their favorite hymns, prayed together and then they all quietly left. The authorities were frustrated with the number of people that showed up for the meeting, and they were somewhat embarrassed also. These Christians are a very peaceful group that have to deal with much persecution throughout the life of this simple house church gathering.

The following Tuesday, May 16, would be a different story. On Monday, May 15, the authorities sealed up the home where the meeting was held each week. They brought in workmen who put up steel doors over the front and rear entrances of the home and then they welded them shut. No one can go in or out. Then they built a brick wall sealing off the main corridor where the many people would have to walk through to get to the meeting. They posted signs up around the home, and also on the main road leading to the home warning people that such meetings are illegal. Then they fingerprinted the homeowner and gave them an official government summons stating a fine of ten thousand YUAN for having a house church meeting in their home. An enormous amount for such simple people. If the fine were only one YUAN it would not be paid.

What is more, then they arrested thirteen people in connection with this meeting and sentenced them to fifteen days in jail. They sought them out, some were arrested at their place of work and some at home. One brother's mother was arrested in order to get to him. They said that she would go free when he was arrested.

In a recent visit to the prison, a sister asked how they were all doing and they responded that they were rejoicing in fellowship, as there are so many Christians together in prison.

Li was not among the thirteen, he is currently at home. He and all the dear believers in Hua Du need prayer for the many decisions that are ahead of them. This simple, peaceful house church meeting has been arbitrarily closed for now.

Pray especially for a brother Yung and Kong.

Encourage your brethren everywhere to pray more for China.

— Douglas

Within the news media and political arenas, there is a growing hostility toward fundamental Christians in the United States who continue to hold to conservative and puritanical ideas. I have heard many ministers express concern about a possible rising Christian persecution in the United States.

Through our movies, television, publications, and the Internet, this nation continues to pollute the world with moral filth. We have more lawyers per capita than any other nation in the world: neighbors sue neighbors, patients sue their doctors, employees sue their employers. The judicial system of the United States has become a quagmire of personal libel and damage cases, while the guilty in many instances are exempt from justice through politically appointed judges or packed juries, the O. J. Simpson case being a prime example.

Even as I finish writing this last chapter, two newsworthy items crossed my desk. One is an Associated Press reported dated June 19, 2000, titled "Court Refuses Evolution Disclaimer," dateline Washington: "The Supreme Court refused to let a public school district require that the teaching of evolution be accompanied by a disclaimer mentioning 'the biblical version of creation' and other teachings on life's origin."

In other words, although evolution is an unproven theory, and teaches without qualification that God (the special Creator as stated in the Bible) did not create anything, and by inference the Bible and the Christian's God is a myth, Christians cannot even tell school children there may be another way of creation. Christians have allowed their children to attend public schools to become the property of those who defy the existence of God.

Another item from the Associated Press, dated June 19, 2000, titled "Court: No Student-Led Prayer at School Sports Events," reports: "The Supreme Court, in the most far-reaching school prayer decision in nearly a decade, ruled Monday that public school districts cannot let students lead stadium crowds in prayer before high school football games." In a dissenting vote, Chief Justice William H. Rehnquist said, "Even more disturbing than its holding is the tone of the court's opinion: it bristles with hostility to all things religious in public life."

Along with these two latest anti-Christian moves by the federal government, the new hate crimes are for the main purpose of getting rid of fundamental and conservative Christians.

As we consider the roster of two hundred nations in the world today, which nation would get the Oscar for its role in Mystery Babylon? It appears the United States would win this dubious award, hands down.

Does America Fit in Revelation 18?

Compare these statements characterizing America with the biblical picture of eschatological Babylon:

1. America exists at the time when Israel becomes a nation (see Jeremiah 50:4–7, 19–20).
2. America's national symbol is the eagle (see Ezekiel 50:4–7, 11–21).

3. America is the greatest economic force in the world and the largest consumer nation (see Revelation 18:11, 15).

4. America's military defense will reach to the heavens (Star Wars technology), but will not deliver her from destruction (see Jeremiah 51:53).

5. America is a nation of mingled people (see Jeremiah 50:37).

6. America is a golden cup with the Lord's hand — a nation He has prospered (see Jeremiah 51:7).

7. America trusts in her own image and knowledge (see Revelation 18:7; Isaiah 47:10).

8. America has become a land given to idolatry (see Jeremiah 50:38; 51:17–18, 47, 52).

9. America has become a land given over to the occult, witchcraft, and sorceries (see Isaiah 47:9, 12–13).

10. America is a nation to which many have come (see Jeremiah 51:44).

11. America's immorality (movies, videos, pornography) has spread corruption throughout the whole earth (see Revelation 18:3).

" . . . Yet forty days, and Nineveh shall be overthrown" (Jonah 3:4). Nineveh repented.

"Repent ye therefore, and be converted, that your sins may be blotted out, when the times of refreshing shall come from the presence of the Lord; And he shall send Jesus Christ, which before was preached unto you" (Acts 3:19–20). Israel did not repent.

"If my people, which are called by my name, shall humble themselves, and pray, and seek my face, and turn from their wicked ways; then will I hear from heaven, and will forgive their sin, and will heal their land" (2 Chron. 7:14).

Whether the United States will be the Mystery Babylon of Revelation 18 does not depend upon the economy; it does not depend upon any politician or political party; it does not depend upon churches filled with professing Christians. It depends upon real Christians who love God, the called according to His purpose, praying and crying out to God to save our nation. It is that simple.

 **Dr. Noah W. Hutchings** serves as president of Southwest Radio Church in Oklahoma City, Oklahoma. He has been with the ministry since April 1951, the same year he received Jesus Christ as Savior and Lord. He has written more than one hundred books and booklets covering Bible commentary and prophetic topics. A member of the board of deacons of the Council Road Baptist Church of Bethany, Oklahoma, Dr. Hutchings is also a member of the University of Biblical Studies in Oklahoma City, and is a member of the Gideons organization.